Making Dollars
while
Making Change

Making Dollars

while

Making Change

The Playbook for Game Changers

Jonathan Quarles

BMcTALKS Press
4980 South Alma School Road
Suite 2-493
Chandler, Arizona 85248

Disclaimer: This book is for educational purposes only. The views expressed are those of the author alone and should not be taken as expert instruction or commands. The reader is responsible for his or her own actions. Adherence to all applicable laws and regulations, including international, federal, state, and local governing professional licensing, business practices, advertising, and all other aspects of doing business in the United States, Canada, or any other jurisdiction is the sole responsibility of the purchaser or reader. Neither the author nor the publisher assumes any responsibility or liability whatsoever on the behalf of the purchaser or reader of these materials.

The views expressed in this publication are those of the author; are the responsibility of the author; and do not necessarily reflect or represent the views of BMcTALKS Press, its owner, or its contractors.

Volume pricing is available to bulk orders placed by corporations, associations, and others. For details, please contact BMcTALKS Press at info@bmtpress.com

FIRST EDITION

Library of Congress Control Number: 2020912312

ISBN: 978-1-7351192-3-6

Printed in the United States of America.

To my beautiful daughters Bella, Jai, and Emerson,
the inspiration for this project:
You have repurposed my life and given me
the strength and courage to be my best, highest self.

Special Thanks

Stella Binkevich
Tavis Smiley
Dr. Na'im Akbar

Contents

Foreword

Doing well and doing good are not antithetical concepts. One can both prosper and serve people if one has a heart full of grace and a soul generated by love.

Jonathan Quarles is such a man. A man who I have known since he was a young boy. Over the years, I have watched him lead, love, save, and serve.

As a teenager, Jonathan was actively involved in my foundation's Youth 2 Leaders program where we taught young people about the real meaning of servant leadership: "You can't lead people if you don't love people, and you can't save people if you don't serve people."

Jonathan let these words sink into his soul, as I have watched his work and witness throughout time with pride and joy.

Making Dollars While Making Change is a testament to how our values help to determine our value, how our roots help to determine our routes.

Each of us has a story. I believe that reading Jonathan's story can help inspire you to start living a life and leaving a legacy—to make dollars while making change.

In his book, Jonathan shares his thinking and, more important, his praxis for using entrepreneurship as a platform for social impact, as a force for good.

Entrepreneurs aren't born, they are made. Jonathan is Flint made—raised in a small town in Michigan that would become a symbol of government negligence years later, when the city inscrutably allowed lead-poisoned water into homes, creating a massive public health crisis.

And yet, this same city of Flint, Michigan would also become a symbol of peace and unity amid the protests and turmoil following the death of George Floyd. The good people of Flint know a little something about never letting misery have the last word—something every entrepreneur needs to understand and embrace, a topic that Jonathan beautifully unpacks throughout this text.

He also discusses how to make the most of your time, how to attract your network as opposed to the all-too-common advice about how to build it, how to foster sustainable relationships, when and how to strike out on your own, and the art and science of navigating the intersection of entrepreneurship and social change.

When I first met Jonathan in Chicago many years ago, he was but one young person in an auditorium full of young people, all anxious to learn how to use their gifts and talents to make a difference in their communities. And, yet, from the moment I met him, Jonathan stood out. I knew he was going to do great things.

Since game recognizes game, I would be lying if I said that any of Jonathan's business success, from his holding company, The BTL Group, to Quartz Water Source, his latest venture, is a surprise. I didn't just hope for it, I expected it.

And that's what makes the difference.

Expectation.

Claiming things that are not, as though they already were.

See it. Believe it. Achieve it.

That's what Jonathan did, and you can too.

Making Dollars While Making Change.

Go ahead, start reading.

Tavis Smiley
Los Angeles, California
July 2020

Chapter 1
Flint Made

Lord, we know what we are, but know not what we may be.
—Ophelia, *Hamlet*, Act IV, Scene V
William Shakespeare

The heat was blazing, the humidity was high, and the wind was cool and swift. The sound of loud, old-school, hip hop music blasting through the speakers filled the streets. Gang members were posted on their respective corners selling drugs, monitoring the streets, and holding it down, as they would say. It was a normal summer day for my twelve-year-old self.

Ron, my best friend, and I decided to stop at the corner store on our way to my house. He got his usual bag of Hot Cheetos. I got my favorite grape juice box with the aluminum peel top. We exchanged a few jokes with the slick-talking, nontraditional Arab owner, then headed toward the door. Before my boy could reach for the door handle, he was staring down the barrel of a twelve-gauge rifle.

I immediately froze, everything around me becoming a blur at once. The only thing I could see was the finger that controlled the trigger. The juice box fell out of my hand, hitting the floor, as my heartbeat grew louder. The rushing sound of the bullet roaring through the chamber and firing out of the clip overpowered my ears. Blood splattered in all directions as I watched my best friend fall to the floor.

I could hear a deep, demanding voice crying out for help, but my body wasn't responding nor was my mind processing the words being yelled in my direction. My response wasn't simply delayed; it was non-existent. I was stuck. Lifeless. Just like my friend. Then I looked at the trigger finger and it was my turn to stare down the barrel of that twelve-gauge rifle. I slowly closed my eyes and exhaled. That moment changed my life forever.

Growing up in the inner city of Flint, Michigan, was amazing through the eyes of a young, black boy. I lived in the heart of the city and my heart was in it. Our community was established by retired homeowners of Caucasian and African American descent, which made growing up enjoyable and safe. I was raised on Mount Elliott Avenue, in a big, white house on a hill, according to my youthful, yet limited perspective.

It was the house that my parents worked so hard to call their own and that carried all the memories of the Quarles family. The porch had a "Q" on the fence of its entrance to signify our last name. Our home was defined by deeply rooted principles of love, family, and spirituality, all of which helped shape my personal values as a child and as an adult. These principles were embodied and modeled by the three most important people in my life—my granny, my mother, and my father.

The world knew my granny as Lizzie, but I knew her as Granny. She was my very own valentine, born on Valentine's

4

Day. She was the matriarch of our family, the one who kept us together and strong through the tough times. She was tough because tough was all she knew how to be. Born and raised in Arkansas, my granny lost her mother at the age of five. Her father remarried a vile, mean-spirited, and abusive woman who helped raise my granny and her siblings.

Her rugged childhood made her a steadfast, decisive, and fearless woman. The kind of woman who worked long hours at Buick City in Flint to provide her children with a life different from her own. For someone with no formal education, she was so strategic and meticulous about her finances that she died having paid off her house, with no debt, and with life insurance policies for the entire family.

My granny possessed a sharp business intuition that influenced generations after her. Although she willingly cooked for the neighborhood and still had leftovers for her family, she was also the grandmother who did not suffer fools gladly when it came to her family, especially her grandchildren. She had a swift tongue that could cut deep like a knife, and she was willing to fight for those she loved on any given day. As a child, I gave my granny hell with my boyish, curious ways, but I wish she were here to see the man I've become. I wish she were here to see the piece of her that I carry within.

My mother, Ruthy Quarles, was the religious, nurturing, and God-fearing balance of the family, with a comforting touch felt and remembered by everyone with whom she interacted. She was born in Flint, Michigan, to a young mother who birthed her at the age of nineteen and essentially raised her as a single parent. My grandmother masterfully struck the balance between being a guardian and being my mom's genuine best friend. With the arrival of my mom's closest sibling a whopping seventeen years later, she unexpectedly became a secondary mother figure to him and three other siblings over time, resulting in the sacrifice of her own childhood, but bringing her even closer to my grandmother. My mom was raised in a huge family and a household that bustled with siblings, cousins, aunts, and uncles, a family structure and a home set-up that might feel familiar to many readers of color.

She brought her close-knit family upbringing into our immediate family, alongside her principles of respect, love, and spirituality. As a woman of faith, my mother strived to satisfy God and influenced her family to do the same. She lived a smoke-free and alcohol-free life, never succumbing to the temptations of her environment. She personified virtuousness in a way that constantly made me think twice, sometimes three times, before doing something that I knew I had no business doing. Her spirit was beautiful, her love unconditional, and I always felt both despite the rebellious nature of my behavior growing up.

Bill Quarles, my father and hero, is the man who led our household and set the example of manhood, hard work, and sacrifice. My father was the first person to expose me to the concept of ownership and to the benefits of working for your last name, not your first name. He was the perfect father for raising strong, black boys. He was an ethical, detail-oriented, strategic planner and a lifelong learner with an inspiring work ethic. His drive stemmed from a childhood that prematurely forced him into adulthood for survival.

He was the oldest of his siblings and looked to as the man of the house because of his father's absence. At the age of eight, he dedicated himself to helping his single mother by getting his first job picking cotton. By twelve, he was working as a truck driver for potato companies. He continued to work menial jobs through his young adulthood until an influential encounter with a dentist caused him to become fixated on that career path. He later enrolled at Southern Illinois University, where he was allowed to pay for his education over time. Unfortunately, his dream of becoming a dentist came to a halt because after finishing college, he came to Flint, where there were no dental schools, to find his birth father and stayed there to develop a relationship with him. But not going to dental school did not stop him from working.

My father was a man of all trades. There was nothing that he could not or would not do to provide for his family. I watched him hustle through different jobs, but I never connected his ambition to the struggles of the deindustrializing city around us. I connected it to the expected hustle of a man. From a young age, he told me that I wasn't born to be average. I was uniquely great with a divine mission that would become bigger than I could ever imagine.

Because of this, he named me Jonathan, a biblical name that means God's gift. I was the one son, out of his three, that he said he never worried about. Even when I was in and out of trouble, he never worried. He saw a lot of himself in me. The only difference between him and me was that I was raised by him. I had a father—my mentor, my protector, and my priest. I had a powerful influence who would become the driving force of my journey to success.

Despite the idealism of my younger years, I now know that my family wasn't well off. But as short as we may have been on financial resources, I never felt like I didn't have something I wanted. On the days that my parents couldn't feed us, we would visit my granny or an aunt, both of whom had a delicious meal waiting no matter the time of day or the circumstances. Whatever we lacked in money, we made up for in gratitude, resourcefulness, and patience.

As I matured, my eyes slowly began to open to the realities of living in Flint. The neighborhood that I once knew as peaceful and safe became one of the most dangerous places on the map. After a series of layoffs at General Motors causing homeowners to vacate, drugs and gangs became my neighborhood's new tenants. Even school didn't always feel safe. Funding palpably decreased due to the thinning real estate tax base, exponentially driving up the ratio of students to teachers. My peers and I felt increasingly more comfortable misbehaving. Our classmate, Michael, would bring lunch from Arby's, a fast-food restaurant, where his mom worked as a waitress. Even though my parents gave me lunch every day, I found myself wanting more, so I would persistently steal that of Michael. One day, Michael pulled a knife on me in an attempt to retaliate. I fearlessly chased Michael for blocks despite that knife. After that incident, my third grade teacher at the time warned me that I was either going to end up dead or in jail, and the truth is the odds weren't in my favor. Limited resources, heightened crime, and elevated unemployment rates became frequent headlines in the Flint local news.

The night's silence became loud, and the sound of spiraling gunshots through the dark sky became our new norm. The lack of visible and accessible influences in business, medicine, law, and other professions compelled me to admire what I was exposed to—drug dealers, hustlers, and gangsters. Although their purpose was deemed unlawful, it was their dedication to maintaining the flow of money, loyalty, and honor that I respected.

The drastic change in the economy caused most of our longtime neighbors to flee the neighborhood, but my parents were determined to stay. Together, they stood behind the mindset that nobody was going to run them out of their home. They were firmly established in Flint and staying through rough times would only build character. Inevitably, my father hustled harder and, as always, I aspired to emulate his behavior.

My journey in entrepreneurship began when I was about eight years old. I was a paperboy for the local newspaper, running early morning routes before the sun came up. In hindsight, it was not the ideal first job. The early mornings were dreadful. The door-to-door sales were a door slam away from traumatizing. The long, chilly rides were enough to make me want to flatten both tires. And the roll-and-rubber-band routine was beginning to cause signs of early carpal tunnel. It wasn't until I inherited an additional route that I saw an opportunity for growth.

After a boy in the neighborhood quit, my territory tripled, making me responsible for more than I could handle alone. Instead of being the next one to quit, I decided to build a team. I recruited a few kids from the neighborhoods within each area to complete the routes. I recruited others to roll and rubber band the newspapers in the morning for the route runners. In exchange, I gave all of them a percentage of my rate. Within days, I had a fully functioning and productive paper route business.

On many mornings, the job was a struggle, but it was memorable and influential because of the valuable lessons that followed. It taught me how to problem-solve, recruit, negotiate, create systems, and prioritize. More important, it helped me develop a good work ethic and a fascination with being my own boss. It took a lot of discipline to get up at five o'clock in the morning without the motivation of a bacon-and-egg aroma. In hindsight, that motivation was tied to a rewarding feeling about making my own money and it stuck with me for a long time.

After my paperboy experience, I tried my hand at a different kind of paper business. While watching my father generate payroll documents and business templates with his first color-ink printer, I quickly became intrigued and convinced him to teach me what he knew. I took his training and started a full-service printing company. I offered my services to the teachers at school, using my self-made business cards to market low prices and quick turnaround times for their ice cream social and book fair needs. Before I knew it, orders were coming in, and money was flowing.

My next business venture stemmed from an in-school student problem. In the fourth grade, our vending machines broke, causing a huge uproar among the students. With the money that I made from the printing company, I purchased candy bars by the bulk and sold them at a 50 percent markup. After a week of selling out daily, I assessed my inventory, identified my best sellers, and restocked. I continued to sell out daily until I graduated from sixth grade. I brought the same mindset to middle school.

My T-shirt business jump-started at the beginning of sixth grade in ways that I didn't necessarily expect. It began by talking to Woody, the son of the owner of Greene Home for Funerals, where my dad was employed at the time. The curious kid who saw an opportunity to organize an additional newspaper route decided to pick Woody's brain about how the T-shirts were made. I didn't have the vocabulary then but, looking back on it, I was really asking about operating costs, retail price, and profit. He didn't give me much, but I quickly connected the dots on the brief rundown that he did give. If my friends and I were that excited about these custom T-shirts, I thought, there must be plenty of others who would share our sentiment.

Once again, I started by building a team. This time, I recruited a few friends to handle the T-shirt designs and hot press screening. I, on the other hand, focused on developing a price list that would cover the cost of printing and allow the operation to make money. I also helped us advertise by talking to everyone I could find (not much has changed) and by dropping flyers all over the school—the likes of an advertising plan devised by an eleven-year-old before the internet boom and the age of social media. Demand skyrocketed. In a matter of weeks, I was running a full-service T-shirt company. We even shipped a few batches to folks outside of Flint.

The last venture I focused on before heading to high school was a janitorial enterprise inspired by the time I spent with my dad. Besides working as a mortician at Greene Home for Funerals, my dad was often given an opportunity to come in before the sun rose and make additional income by cleaning the inside and surrounding area. My brother and I were my father's rather obvious and painfully free choice of help.

I resented the first time he dragged us but felt accomplished when we managed to clean the entire front landscape of the trash and weeds covering it, while my father tended to his duties. Somewhere in the process, I must have realized that creating a comfortable physical space for community members to mourn their loved ones was important, and we got personal recognition from Mr. Greene, the owner.

As I saw the value in our work, my wheels started to turn on another idea—doing this on a weekly basis, for predictable cash flow. I also remember thinking that I didn't enjoy Mr. Greene's ability to call the shots on pricing—I wanted to be able to do that for my services provided. So I spent a few days giving shape to a more formalized verbal business proposal—Mr. Greene surprisingly accepted with no hesitations. Before we knew it, we had a janitorial business on our hands.

While financially, I was prospering, socially, I was struggling. The gangs who infiltrated my neighborhood made it hard for me to walk my normal twenty-minute route to the bus that took me to Sobey, a school on the east side of Flint. Walking turned into running; harsh words turned into fist blows, and long stares turned into black eyes. At the time, my only logical resolution was to join them, for protection, and to partake in the things I feared.

I knew that being part of a gang would enable me to walk those blocks to the bus in peace. I also knew that if my peace was messed with, an army would come to my defense. My parents were unaware that their fourth-grade baby boy was a gang affiliate, and I did my best to keep it that way. I maintained my grades, completed my chores, and obeyed my curfew.

On the other side of that, I threw up gang signs, repped one color, jumped people for no reason, and let curse words roll off my tongue like a sailor. I had a front-row seat to drugs, guns, violence, and alcohol. Most people would attribute what I did to peer pressure, but in reality, I joined first and my friends followed.

Although I had a gift for turning products into profits, there was always a side of me that loved to fight, which made gang affiliation more intriguing. Because guns and drugs were off limits for the younger gang members, I got a chance to show off my skills in street fighting. If it wasn't active fighting, it was hanging out and keeping the peace between territories. Even though gang culture contributed to the negative image of the city that I loved, my gang affiliation turned into yet another business lesson.

My up-close-and-personal view of organized criminal activity gave me insight into the organization of people, leadership, system development, money management, and a product supply chain. From the outside looking in, most people saw crime, but I saw a structured, well-functioning business. I saw an opportunity to take unlawful, yet successful, business principles, and apply them to a legal enterprise. What I did not see was the spirit of death.

After watching a single gunshot claim my close friend's life while buying grape juice, I knew that my gang affiliation had to come to an end. The finger on that trigger threatened me into silence about what happened and left me with the responsibility of explaining my friend's death to his mother. I had to explain why the blood that seeped through my shirt and sprinkled across my face belonged to him and not me. I had to explain how I left with him and came back without him. I had to explain why a twelve-year-old boy became a singled-out victim at a corner store. More important, I had to explain why his life was taken, not mine.

Fear kept me silent. Looking through his mother's red-toned, tearful, pain-filled eyes didn't break me. The fear was stronger. To this day, I can't explain why my life was spared, but it was, and it gave me a second chance to get it right. I knew that my constant street fighting wasn't living up to the way that my parents raised me nor was it a reflection of my core values. I would constantly imagine my parents' pain if they learned that I was murdered—the dreadful visions were another incentive to clean up my act and take the universe up on the second chance to be a good citizen.

I initiated a jump out, the process of disassociating from a gang. I retained my fighting spirit but channeled it toward more positive influences. When the jump out was over, I didn't complain about my busted lip, sore ribs, or black eyes. From a young age, I've always been one to peacefully live with the ramifications of my decisions. Plus, I'd seen worse.

I simply turned the moment into motivation to change and to do things my way. I began filling my time with sports; I focused on getting better grades; and I steeped myself in public school activities like the science fair, a place where you would've never caught me before.

Chapter 2

The Makings of an Entrepreneur

But you are a chosen generation, a royal priesthood, a holy nation, His own special people, that you may proclaim the praises of Him who called you out of darkness into His marvelous light.

—1 Peter 2:9

It was 1998, and I was a sophomore in high school with my own television show that focused on youth leadership development. It aired on Flint's local public network three times per week for the remainder of my high school years. As the producer and host, I had four students working with me to create and direct content.

At the time, Tavis Smiley was on Black Entertainment Television (BET) with his namesake program, *The Tavis Smiley Show*, which I would watch for inspiration every night. His dedication to developing young black leaders quickly turned me into a fan and gave me a ton to consider for my show. More important, Tavis had a profound impact on me throughout my high school years because both his values and his journey as a young person had a comforting resemblance to those of my father. His rhetoric and actions about the principles of business ownership, community service, and advocating for the voiceless were powerful and familiar, albeit from a distance.

In the summer of 2000, Tavis Smiley started Youth 2 Leaders, a program that taught young people about the importance of service. Back then information wasn't as easily accessible as it is today. But in a fortunate twist of fate, I learned that there would be Youth 2 Leaders summits in Detroit; Chicago; Philadelphia; Atlanta; Los Angeles; and Washington, DC. The summit consisted of a free day of programming in which young, black Americans, ages fourteen to eighteen, were given a framework to think about the systemic issues plaguing their communities and to design solutions for them together. To me, this was the perfect opportunity to meet Tavis and convince him to let me shadow. Unfortunately, I missed the Detroit Summit, scheduled for June 24, but was relieved to learn that Chicago was Tavis's next step. Without hesitation, I applied for the Chicago summit, got accepted, and made arrangements for the four-hour drive down I-94 to meet someone I considered a giant.

Throughout the leadership summit, I made sure to ask thoughtful questions and engage as many participants as possible with the hopes of forging relationships with like-minded youth throughout the Midwest. At the end of the summit, Tavis announced that there would be auditions for a panel discussion with State Senator Barack Obama and Congressman Jesse Jackson, Jr.

There were only two slots on the panel for summit partici-pants—instantaneously, I decided that one of them would belong to me. Learning the power of visualization at an early age, I imagined myself on that stage. I knew that securing a slot on this panel would be my golden ticket to meeting and impressing Tavis Smiley, and I had a plan to do just that.

Both Tavis and his team observed me working the room and leading in discussions throughout the day, which made my name a unanimous vote when it came to the slot selection process. My community activism in Flint also impressed him and the other political figures. After the panel discussion, I turned a picture-taking, small-talk moment into an elevator pitch for my vision of working with Tavis.

Prior to attending the conference, I did some research and discovered that he was looking for long-term national sponsors to support his foundation. Armed with that information, I proposed to serve as the first youth ambassador for his foundation, succinctly explaining why I was uniquely positioned to be a poster child for his work when it came to prospective sponsors and donors.

The two minutes of consideration that he gave my proposal were two more minutes than I ever expected. I felt a mix of pride and affirmation as Tavis connected me to Andrea Foggy-Paxton, the executive director of the Tavis Smiley Foundation at the time. From that moment on, Andrea was the bottleneck in my quest to become the first youth ambassador for Tavis Smiley's Youth 2 Leaders program.

After twenty persistent phone calls and emails to Foggy-Paxton's office, Jonathan Quarles became a household name for the folks who worked at the foundation. They knew that this young, relentless kid from Flint, Michigan, was willing to move heaven and earth to convince Andrea that he was meant to be the first youth ambassador.

My upbringing in Flint seeded me with a sense of grit and gave me the tools to persevere in the midst of challenges. To some, Flint's journey from being a haven of the Great Migration to a widely cited example of the manufacturing downturn might have been a history lesson, but for my family, it was a trying, lived experience.

Nevertheless, my parents, along with most Flint residents, knew how to take lemons and make the most flavorful lemonade that's ever been made. In difficult moments, they knew how to lean on what was important—family, community, and the vibrant human spirit that was so alive, despite Flint's circumstances. From an early age, I've felt a responsibility to tell Flint's story and to carry the average residents of the city on my shoulders. Being a youth ambassador for Tavis felt like a perfect platform to do that.

Smiley's staff in Los Angeles not only knew my name, but also recognized my voice because I showered the office with calls on weekdays and weekends. The foundation was closed on Sundays, but I still left messages. The staff was so accustomed to my routine phone calls that, if I missed a day, they would joke about it the next time we talked, saying something like, "We thought you gave up on us!" Even though my initial efforts didn't yield the result I wanted, giving up was not an option. I just needed a different approach.

One Saturday morning, while waiting for a haircut at Mack's Barbershop, I was flipping through a stack of *Ebony* and *Jet* magazines and stumbled on an article about the inaugural State of the Black Union. It was being organized on the University of Southern California's campus in Los Angeles and hosted by Tavis Smiley.

On Monday, I rang the Tavis Smiley Foundation at six A.M. Pacific Standard Time, determined to be the first call they received. I spoke to the chief operating officer and executive advisor, Denise Pines, who had first mistaken me for the news outlet that Tavis was doing an interview with that morning. I capitalized on her excitement and confusion to squeeze my interest into the conversation, but she recognized my name from prior communication attempts and laughed. I was unequivocal in relaying my enthusiasm about attending Tavis's State of the Black Union as a volunteer, at my expense.

Within twenty-four hours, I received an email informing me that the Tavis Smiley Foundation would honor my request to be a volunteer, cover my travel expenses, and provide me lodging for the event. I was ecstatic. It felt like Christmas had come early and Santa only brought gifts for me.

My experience at the State of the Black Union with Tavis was my first, and most unforgettable, window into how the worlds of business, politics, art, and sports intersect. A relentless "country boy" from Flint, I was suddenly mingling with the individuals who defined the culture that shaped me, and it felt like a dream. My trip to Los Angeles also re-affirmed the importance of persistence and the power of imagination. I recognized that persistence led me to this un-believable opportunity of working with a man whom I previously only knew and admired through a television screen.

Imagining the opportunity before it happened led to Tavis Smiley finally rolling the dice and taking me on as his first youth ambassador. That role opened incredible doors, giving me a chance to interact with State Senator Barack Obama, Congressman Jesse Jackson Jr., and many others of similar stature, putting me on a path to a stronger, more diverse network than I could've ever fathomed.

Establishing a chapter of Students Against Violence Everywhere (S.A.V.E) at my high school sophomore year was another defining experience. The constant reckless loss of lives in Flint had a compounding mental impact on me and my peers. I had also experienced a direct loss in my family. I distinctly remember a birthday party that my favorite uncle, Bow Bow, did not attend after never having missed any of my special occasions. The next day we found out that Uncle Bow Bow was dead—he had been murdered in his own home. As I digested his death many years later, coupled with that of my best friend, Ron, I needed an outlet, and S.A.V.E. was it. In many ways, S.A.V.E. saved me from what felt like soul-crushing pain at the time. S.A.V.E. gave students a platform to raise awareness about gun and gang violence. Our chapter was overseen by the memorable Mr. Young, a teacher who would put you in your place quicker than you knew where your place was. S.A.V.E. also fund-raised to enable families with no money to hold funerals for their loved ones and to get them counseling in the aftermath of loss. My chapter grew to be between three and four hundred people, becoming the largest in the country. S.A.V.E. became a place of healing for me and many others and a great training ground for communication, capital procurement, and organizing.

As I headed into my junior year, my dad made it clear that I was going to college and that it wasn't a choice. It was like the last act in his rite of passage to manhood for each of his three boys. Not only was I going to college, he told me, but I would also be the one paying for it with either a job or scholarship funds. With that in mind, I spent the next two years focused on academics, sports, and my game plan to obtain as many scholarships for college as possible.

I used Jeremiah, my middle brother, as a blueprint for my scholarship efforts by creating an inventory that started with the scholarships he applied for, and adding many others. I assessed the final inventory and generated a systematic game plan to apply for over 100 scholarships between then and the end of high school, including scholarships that I did not qualify for based on their requirements. My business-oriented mind saw this as a numbers game.

Every evening, after finishing my homework, I scheduled a block of time to research, file, and identify the most commonly sought-after qualifications in scholarship applications. My goal was to understand these qualifications and use them to strategically select my extracurricular activities and leadership positions. After two years of executing on my evening routine, I achieved my goal in applying for 112 scholarships, resulting in just north of $100,000 in scholarship funds. My academic achievements earned me admissions to several schools, each accompanied by fully-paid tuition, leaving me with over $100,000 to spend however I deemed. This was a turning point in the trajectory of my life—the access to capital from scholarships enabled me to start building wealth.

As nervous as I might have been to leave Flint, Florida Agricultural and Mechanical University (FAMU), a historically black university in Tallahassee, Florida, quickly became my new home. I entered the School of Business and Industry as a sophomore after transferring college credits earned at the University of Michigan-Flint in high school.

I lived in a scholarship house with seventeen intelligent, young men who shared my skin color but came from completely different cultures. Some flew across oceans and had roots in Haiti, The Bahamas, Trinidad, Honduras, Nigeria, and England. Others were from cities within the US like New Orleans, Chicago, Pensacola, Miami, Brooklyn, and Los Angeles. Coming from sharing one bathroom with three people to sharing a bathroom with seventeen strangers was an unexpected and challenging adjustment. It took some time, but my adaptive personality eventually learned to embrace the crowd.

Out of the seventeen students, I grew close to one. His name was Ade and he came to FAMU all the way from Nigeria. He was a double major in computer science and electrical engineering. I was intrigued by his independence, maturity, and work ethic. He seemed to handle his first day at FAMU alone, stoically. He didn't have the luxury of his parents walking him through the campus, taking part in orientation, or helping him unpack. They weren't around to meet his new roommates or to shower him with the kind of smothering love that only families know how to give. I was lucky to have all of the above.

When school started, we were complete opposites. He was an introverted student who studied constantly and seemed entirely unfazed by the new frontier of social life that college had to offer. I was an extrovert who prioritized my academics and business gigs during the day but partied frequently and voraciously at night. Based on our personalities alone, we could've lived parallel lives, but our love for food brought us together.

The aroma of Nigerian food permeating through the house turned my curiosity into a taste test. I remember trying jollof rice for the first time. One taste test turned into frequent meals during which Ade taught me about Nigerian culture through his cooked food. Frequent meals instantly took our conversations beyond food and culture to random boy talk and time-tested life lessons.

In exchange for his well-seasoned jollof rice with a side of Nigerian culture, I taught Ade how to drive. And though it took two years, I also taught him how to enjoy the social benefits of college without sacrificing his academic responsibilities. My friendship with Ade was the first that I had ever developed with someone who was a native of Africa, my elusive ancestral home, and I was enthralled.

Not only did I realize that his personality was a great counterbalance to mine, but Ade also influenced a lot more than my diverse taste buds. Our relationship served as the foundation for my understanding of the global nature of the world. I was inspired to travel to the motherland, a place that had only existed in my imagination until Ade. FAMU's Office of International Education and Development offered programs in South Africa, Japan, and South America—I chose South Africa without any hesitation.

In 2003, I crossed the Atlantic Ocean to immerse myself in a completely different reality. It was my first trip outside the US, and it was eye-opening. I studied finance at the University of Johannesburg. I focused on my studies during the day and spent the afternoons wandering the nearby neighborhoods tasting organic, earth-grown foods. The fried and processed foods that I was accustomed to were nowhere to be found, so I had to learn to love fresh food.

I also had the opportunity to meet the US ambassador to South Africa, Lana Marks. The role of an ambassador had never been on my radar until that moment, but I left the interaction increasingly fascinated with the way it intersected business, human behavior, and politics. I tacitly placed pursuing the position on my constantly growing, but intentional, list of long-term aspirations.

On the weekends, I traveled to neighboring countries. I visited Zimbabwe, Namibia, and Botswana, allowing me to experience the changing cultural terrain, the healthy cultural competition among African countries, and the ubiquitous wealth disparities that plagued almost every nation that I experienced on the African continent. I was on the other side of the globe, but the wealthy, metropolitan areas in all these countries bore more resemblance to cities in Florida and Texas than to villages in Africa. This helped me understand just how far-reaching the tentacles of Western colonization were.

Good, bad, and ugly, studying abroad was the first time that I felt proverbially at home—like there was an inextricable link between my identity and the people and cultures that I encountered, albeit varied. It was a spiritual transformation, and I returned to the US a different person. My homeland was no longer just a figment of my imagination. It was real. I had walked its streets and taken in its sights, smells, and sounds. I had a broader understanding of where I came from, which strengthened me for the journey ahead.

Inside the classroom, I learned the art of business from professors who were actual industry practitioners. They were business owners and entrepreneurs, which, in my opinion, differentiated FAMU's business school at the time from many others. Outside the classroom, the diversity of my scholarship house continued to afford me learning that was often far more valuable than my learning within. Implicitly, I was being exposed to the principles that underlie doing business across cultures, to real estate, to investing, and to entrepreneurship. My living situation was a perfect training ground for internalizing that, no matter the business or the goal, trust and cultural awareness had to come first. I've returned to this principle, time and time again, in the years since I was at FAMU.

I recall overhearing a side conversation between house-mates, who were joking about portfolios. At first, I was thoroughly confused because my then understanding of portfolios was limited to a three-ring zipper binder with folders. Little did I know that they were conversing about investment portfolios, leading me to recall snippets of overheard conversations between my parents about building wealth through saving. Now I know that the term "portfolio" is used to refer to a series of investments, chosen to offset or amplify each other, depending on which way the market moves, but that is a far way away from where I was then. I've always referred to myself as a "little country boy from Flint," and that was a distinct and memorable moment in which I had to contend with my own ignorance. My peers were playing chess, and I barely knew how to play checkers.

Luckily, within minutes, my housemates welcomed me to the conversation and taught me about the benefits of investing in predeveloped land as one asset in a portfolio. After my own research confirmed their insights, I used a portion of my scholarship money to invest in my first acre of predeveloped land. Over the course of the next three years, I continued to purchase and flip predeveloped land for profitable gains. Knowing that I would, one day, be a father, I set aside a considerable amount of my profits into mutual funds—companies that pool money and invest it in stocks, bonds, and short-term debt—and 529 tuition saving plans—state-sponsored vehicles designed to put money away for college.

Real estate was another hot discussion topic among the business students who made my acquaintance, and before I knew it, real estate became my next venture. The notion of real estate and land ownership as key drivers of wealth building was brought into my consciousness by Dr. Norman Johnson, my accounting professor. With wealth-building as a primary objective, I studied for and passed the Realtor exam while enrolled in the core business curriculum.

Within the year, I obtained my real estate agent license and purchased a three-bedroom, two-bathroom investment property. I began collecting rent on it while living in a scholarship house rent-free, which enabled me to save in the way that I envisioned. I continued to acquire more properties, but my interest in real estate was slowly cannibalized by a desire to hone other skills. I wanted to become meaningfully involved in the FAMU community.

I also went on to start my own premium relationship brokerage firm, Common Link Consulting Services, which provided transformative business advice and political consulting to both for-profit and nonprofit organizations. In the spirit of wanting to be a stakeholder in the decision-making on FAMU's campus, I became a student leader in several organizations, including the Student Government Association, a student-selected body that presided over matters related to student life; the National Association for the Advancement of Colored People (NAACP); and the Presidential Ambassadors. In addition, I joined the distinguished men of the Beta Nu Chapter of Alpha Phi Alpha Fraternity, Incorporated.

I finished my first year with honors, a lucrative real estate investment, and my own business. During the summer, I was fortunate enough to be selected as a Coca-Cola Scholar and given the opportunity to intern at the company's headquarters located in Atlanta, Georgia. I worked for the Coca-Cola Scholars Foundation, identifying and developing strategic partnerships that aligned with Coca-Cola's philanthropic mission, something that companies use to drive the goodwill of customers and shareholders and to have a positive impact in the world. At the time, Coca-Cola was investing resources in grade-school students with academic promise in rural and urban areas to build a pipeline of candidates for its Scholars program.

I was mentored by Ingrid Saunders Jones, then Chair of the Coca-Cola Foundation. She ran all the external relations for North America and I had the pleasure of meeting her during my work with Tavis Smiley. After receiving my internship placement, I requested her as a mentor. She, thankfully, agreed and inquired about what I was seeking to gain from the summer internship. I answered authentically, sharing that I wanted to shadow her and learn as much as possible about how executive decisions are made at the corporate level. Without hesitation, she enabled me to do both. I gained unforgettable firsthand exposure to the financial and managerial operations of a well-known corporation. Ingrid's influence on me far outlasted my summer at the Coca-Cola headquarters.

Growing up, my dad taught me that wherever I worked, the primary goal was to identify the person or people who "control the purse," referring to those who hold decision-making power, and to build an alliance with them. He instructed me to learn everything that they knew and to find or create ways to add value to their professional and/or personal lives. As a Coca-Cola Scholar, I did just that with Ingrid Saunders Jones. I learned everything that I could about her, and how she managed a large, vital part of the corporation. I used my time to cultivate a non-transactional relationship with a respected and highly-ranked person in the building.

My relationship with Ingrid had a ripple effect on my moves when I returned to campus. After recognizing the need for accessible soft drinks in the female dormitories, I used my relationship with Coca-Cola Bottling to secure a vending machine deal for FAMU. I singlehandedly managed all the moving parts of the deal, which gained the interest and attention of the student government. A deal with these many pieces would typically be brokered by a more seasoned professional, but I was bold and resourceful enough to try and succeed. In no time, I became the paid student representative for all intergovernmental relations engagements, lobbying for student issues and interests on behalf of FAMU's student government.

As my tenure at FAMU was coming to an end, I found myself at a real crossroads. I had gotten accepted to Harvard's Kennedy School of Government, which I ambivalently deferred for a year of experience in the real world. I had also played with the idea of going to law school but decided that it didn't align with what I liked to do. I ultimately chose to build on my work with Tavis, a choice about which I have zero regrets. As for FAMU—I left it all on the court.

When I entered college as a first-year student with sophomore credits, I didn't expect to leave an international explorer, investor, or Realtor. I also didn't expect to have forged relationships with high-profile corporate and academic executives. FAMU exceeded my wildest expectations, and I exceeded my own. I entered college as a persistent, young hustler and left a polished entrepreneur.

Chapter 3
Making Each Decade Count

If I could travel back in time and give the working version of myself advice, the first thing I would say is, "Money is ultimately a tool, not your master."

—Jonathan Quarles

After graduating from college, I dove headfirst into the workforce with unrealistic expectations, materialistic motivations, and a misguided sense of ambition. With a Master of Business Administration degree and high-impact internships to brag about, I thought I had it all figured out. Sitting where I was at the time, a few salaried jobs felt like the most important ingredient in my recipe for success and happiness.

But life had a way of illuminating a path better than any coursework could teach me. I spent ten years chasing monetary goals and mistakenly tying them to self-fulfillment. In that decade-long chase, I sacrificed a sense of meaning, but what I learned fundamentally changed my paradigm.

The first decade of my working years (2005 to 2015) was consumed with flawed perceptions of success, measured almost solely by quantifiable wealth. Having emerged from humble beginnings, financial wealth was a warranted pursuit, but I always knew that it didn't fully reflect the values instilled in me by my parents and the Flint community.

I wasn't doing anything that harmed my community, but I wasn't necessarily working to advance it either. Instead, I built on my love for exploring the world, exposing myself to new cultures through travel while expanding my skillset, without intentionally focusing on giving back. My aim was largely self-centered, as I crossed one income-generating goal off the list after another, aggressively adding to the digits in my savings account and planning for a future family.

Despite my gains, the interesting thing about the pursuit of financial wealth was that it never felt like enough. It locked me into a perpetual cycle that started with bank account goals and bled into a vision board suddenly filled with material possessions, requiring more financial wealth. While I succeeded in making more money than I could've ever imagined, I wasn't fully tuned in to the ramifications of being an employee. I hadn't paused to consider the disposability of a salaried position in a looming recession, or the degree to which it can be taken away unexpectedly for other reasons. Internalizing those lessons made my first professional decade transformational.

The Networking Lesson

Tavis Smiley was one of the hardest-working and most well-read men who I've ever had the pleasure of partnering with. His commitment to the black community was unwavering, and his mission of improving it landed him in rooms and circles of politicians, celebrities, community influencers, and corporate executives. As his mentee, I was lucky enough to connect with many of his contacts, seeding the beginning of my own growing rolodex. There wasn't a person of influence who I could not meet or had not met because of my relationship with Tavis. Knowing my great fortune, I guarded my network and never took it for granted.

Working with Tavis gave me insight on how critical the ability to do more with less was to nonprofit organizations with charitable missions, like his foundation. He taught me to be mission-driven and prepared, which he viewed as the two key ingredients in, respectfully but persuasively, asking someone to contribute. Being mission-driven meant doing something for true purpose, not for profit—a concept that, once internalized, meaningfully shaped my outlook on how I wanted to spend my time. Acting with purpose entailed examining what you're doing through the prism of how a history book would describe you and your work—the opposite of "phoning it in."

Knowing how to ask was key, and I learned that concept with hours of practice in my bathroom mirror. I always had a way with words, and after seeing me wax poetic to a room full of corporate executives who were persuaded to support our mission, Tavis coined "JQ Smooth" as my new nickname. I leaned on my gift of persuasion to build long-lasting relationships that would later help me during my transition into corporate America.

The Government Lesson
I will never forget that call from Detroit Mayor Kwame Kilpatrick. It was a brisk December evening in Washington,

DC, and I had just finished my workout at Fitness USA. As I walked out, heading to the metro Red Line, a ring from a 313 area code lit up my screen. I didn't recognize the number, but I answered regardless. A bold, but familiar, voice on the other end said, "Jonathan Quarles, it's Mayor Kwame Kilpatrick."

The voice brought back a flood of memories of interning for him in high school when he was the Michigan House minority whip. Externally, he's six foot five inches tall with two hundred and seventy pounds in body mass. Internally, he was fiercely intelligent, undeniably charismatic, and skilled at articulating a vision and mobilizing around it. As a high schooler, I admired his leadership and worked to forge a relationship that transcended professional interactions.

As luck would have it, we went on to create a deeper, lifelong bond. Kilpatrick influenced my decision to attend FAMU by meaningfully painting his alma mater as a "microcosm of life." Although I intended to pledge Omega Psi Phi Fraternity to continue the legacy of my father and other family members, Kilpatrick was the man who sponsored my decision to join the Beta Nu Chapter of Alpha Phi Alpha Fraternity, Incorporated.

On our call that night, Kilpatrick recalled my interest in community building and in serving my hometown of Flint as its potential mayor. He explained that my affinity for public service, coupled with his recollection of my work ethic, led him to make that phone call inviting me back to his office—this time as a partner in creating a better Detroit.

Newly reelected Mayor Kwame Kilpatrick was familiar with the relationships and the access that I had acquired to both public and private sector leaders through my work with Tavis Smiley. After a tight reelection bid, Kilpatrick understood the political benefits of adding a well-connected senior advisor, like me, to his team.

Despite my tremendous respect and admiration for him, I was hesitant to accept the position. The idea of returning to Michigan and swallowing a sizable pay cut was not exactly in line with my pursuit of financial wealth. But some prayer and a few conversations with mentors later, my doubt turned into a calling. I began to recognize the mutual benefit—the city needed my expertise, and I could gain an insider's understanding of the government sector in my home state.

As his new senior advisor, I was basically Mayor Kilpatrick's gatekeeper. I was responsible for ensuring that I knew everything he knew and was expected to know. I had to be prepared for every meeting, every speech, and every external event. I managed the team who handled his scheduling, mail, communications, and coordinated his strategy execution in partnership with the city's department heads. This was, by far, the most meaningful and impactful position that I've ever had the honor of holding.

Mayor Kwame Kilpatrick was unequivocally one of Detroit's most effective mayors, though he would never get the credit he deserved. Under his leadership, more houses were built in the city than under any previous mayor. He repaired more streets, erected more parks and recreation centers, brought more national events to the city, and created more quantifiable economic development than any previous mayor. Though the city's resources were strained, Mayor Kilpatrick's ability to connect the dots and bring folks along with his vision allowed him to accomplish more than expected. He was always laser focused on the task at hand, which was achieving change for his people. Because of this, he earned my undeniable respect.

While helping improve the lives of Detroit residents through policy, I amassed a large transferable skillset. Observing Kilpatrick, I learned that public service is a calling, not an aspiration. The tenure of those who are not called is typically short-lived and rife with ineffectiveness. Mayor Kilpatrick's calling powered him with an unparalleled intensity, which always put him ten steps ahead of patrons and other stakeholders. I had to match his level of intensity, learning the art and science of government leadership.

Much like Tavis's foundation, we constantly had to figure out how to do more for the community with less—leveraging the power of government was a big component. The power of government, as I came to understand it, was rooted in coalition building and strategic partnerships. I navigated all this to become a deft government operator—a concept that I came to know well during my years with Kilpatrick.

A good operator has to have an intimate understanding of the different aspects of government and be able to flow through them seamlessly without much of a playbook. An operator is responsible for delivering outcomes, while the circumstances of the governmental ecosystem remain ever-changing. Kilpatrick made this an easy skill to pick up because his days were never the same. It wasn't atypical that, on any given day, I was tasked with putting out a public relations fire, balancing a problematic budget, ameliorating friction with city council, and planning meetings with the governor's office that would advance our agenda as opposed to reacting. Over time, the consistent demands forced me to become an expert at getting work done by the right people, at the right time, and in an ethical manner. Consequently, I left the government sector with a just-do-it-and-get-it-done attitude.

Interestingly enough, I also finished my government gig somewhat disillusioned with the system, a feeling that took me years to get rid of. Working for Kilpatrick made me realize that public servants are always being watched and that the scrutiny was even more intense for politicians of color. I don't dissuade anyone from living a life of public service, but I do urge those who want it to carefully think about the path, especially in the age of live videos and social media.

The Corporate Lesson

Tower Defense & Aerospace, LLC, a defense and aerospace firm formerly known as W Industries, was my first full-time stepping-stone in the corporate world. My time in Kilpatrick's administration helped me succeed in this position. While working for the mayor, I made some introductions to Tower Defense & Aerospace that apparently left an impression, because the firm came knocking on my door several months later.

I joined Tower Defense & Aerospace as its chief lobbyist and vice president of new business development. I was Tower's youngest executive, and it was my longest stint in corporate America, until federal budget cuts to defense spending wiped out the business. Before I resigned, I obtained a Lean Six Sigma Black Belt certification, which is given to those who complete a one-year course on creating efficient corporate processes that maximize customer value while minimizing waste, and I went through multiple professional development trainings on the company's budget. At the time, my motivation for seeking the Lean Six Sigma certification was to help bridge the gap between underappreciated workers and misunderstood managers by cutting down on inefficiencies that made everyone work slower. That said, I knew that a year-long training for a well-known certification could potentially come in handy down the line.

Covisint, an information technology company, became my second and final corporate stepping-stone. I worked as the vice president for public sector sales, essentially helping the company go public. Once the company was listed, the chief executive officer (CEO) was fired and replaced with a West Coast executive who had no experience managing the company's business model at the time. Employee morale declined as a result, bringing me to a realization that I no longer wanted to work for an organization that was not challenging or fulfilling. Especially because I had plateaued in growing my corporate skillset, working to fulfill the highly unfulfilling mission of others for relative pennies no longer made sense.

Collectively, my corporate experiences exposed me to a jarring wait-your-turn mentality. On the one hand, my quarterly reviews consistently ranked me above others in quantifiable metrics and managing teams, all while working within ubiquitous budget constraints. Given the positive feedback, I would ask the natural proceeding question,

"When can I be promoted and gain more responsibilities?" To which the corporate powers would always deliver a variation of a well-rehearsed answer, "You are still young; wait your turn. You have many years ahead of you." This answer was not only viscerally inconsistent with my performance reviews, but it was also highly demoralizing. I was bold and outspoken, so some colleagues viewed me as a threat, bringing on more of the same wait-your-turn responses.

I finally left corporate America, but I did so with valuable lessons that still guide how I conduct business. Corporate America taught me that commanding respect was often more valued than quantifiable results, and that honorable conduct was important. Corporate America also helped me understand that people want to feel valued before committing to someone else's vision. Once commitment is secured, building morale among employees and a culture of positivity among customers goes further than a sky-high bottom line.

As one of the youngest senior executives at Tower, a billion-dollar company at the time, I learned that managing over sixty people is more about managing emotions and internal politics, than it was about turning billions into trillions. I often managed employees who were old enough to be my parents, and who had more work experience than I did. Regardless, I had to build the same kind of rapport with them as I did with folks my age. Managing my own emotions in the process was important—I was the youngest and only black executive at the firm. If I got emotional about every slight and negative interaction, it would be very difficult to think straight and make good work-related decisions. Managing the emotions of others meant making them feel heard and doing so with a sincere and open heart. It didn't always mean agreeing or taking a well-liked stance, but it did mean making the space to listen.

My overriding dilemma in all my corporate jobs was always about learning internal politics and meeting company expectations, while maintaining a solid moral compass and my own sense of humanity. Possibly the most important lesson that corporate America taught me was that, over time, I no longer wanted to spend my days navigating this dilemma. It's not typical for most people to describe high-stakes corporate experiences, like running a department or taking a company public, as stepping-stones. But as I reflect on my experiences, they were exactly that. They were my stepping-stones to self-actualization and to defining, not finding, my next job.

The Gravesite Theory

Self-actualization is a complicated thing, but what I've come to realize is that many people never get there. Most spend their lives going through the motions with no real sense of purpose. They find themselves swept into motion by the traditional lifecycle—getting an education, getting a job, having a family, buying a house, working until retirement, and dying. My worst nightmare has always been about going through those motions to build someone else's dream by working nine to five. Although some deviate from the traditional path slightly, the deviation is often too insignificant to align with something bigger and more meaningful to make an impact.

In the gravesite theory, there are three important components—date of birth, date of death, and date of transition. The date of my birth was memorable for my parents, but the date of transition marked the day that I decided to focus on creating a legacy for my family. I finally understood that building generational wealth was the bedrock of that legacy, but only as a means of making a greater impact on the world. In the words of Jay-Z, "I can't help the poor if I'm one of them." With that statement in mind, I set out to eradicate poverty across the globe through entrepreneurship.

In hindsight, I wasn't necessarily sure how I would work toward an order that tall. But I did close my corporate decade with some guiding principles to adhere to as I blazed the trail ahead. The first was about my relationship to money. The decade began with delusions of grandeur about just how much money can do. My experiences highlighted that while money can create access, "buy" time otherwise spent on menial tasks, and allow people to invest in others, it cannot and should not bring fulfillment. Money was ultimately a tool and not the master.

The second was about work ethic, something that I saw and valued in my father from a young age. While I was blessed with high emotional intelligence and a nimble sense of adaptability, I was not necessarily the smartest guy in the room. Quickly, I realized that innate talent would only get me so far, but work ethic would get me further. There and then, I committed to an unmatched work ethic that I've leaned on time and again.

The third was about how I made mistakes. Strategic planning was undeniably important, and in my early years, I'd plan until I was blue in the face. I would do this only to realize that it still wasn't possible to anticipate every permutation and that, at some point, I had to relinquish control to the universe. I've found that the more comfortable I became with this notion, the more unafraid I was to make the aggressive bets of an entrepreneur. Aggressive bets did come with aggressive mistakes, and those mistakes did hurt. But there was equal amount of beauty in going for something with all that I had and in the long-lasting learning that resulted from it.

Led by these principles, I set my sights on using entrepreneurship to move the needle on poverty.

Chapter 4
Don't Build Your Network. Attract It.

I did it by knowingly and unknowingly investing in being the best version of myself. This has attracted my network, NOT built it.

—Jonathan Quarles

One of the areas that I've often been asked about is the process by which I built my network. It's a natural question because I worked for two individuals with high name recognition, and I founded my entire consulting business, The BTL Group, on connecting dots and managing relationships for clients. Let me confess that many of my prior answers to this question have fallen short of thoughtful. They've run a generic gamut between surface-level statements and self-deprecating deflections of the core question—"It just comes naturally" or "I adapt to the environment."

As I write this chapter, the entire world is contending with the 2019 coronavirus disease (COVID-19), a time that I believe will bend the arc of history beyond ways that we can imagine. COVID-19 has also been a sacred space for a first-time author like me. It's given me an unprecedented opportunity to reflect on my life, my vision for this book, and on what I'd like to impart to you, the reader.

I want to dedicate this chapter to actually unpacking how my network came to be, and to doing justice to those who have been brave enough to ask for prescriptive advice. The self-discovery detailed here has made for a long and winding road, some of which has taken upward of two decades. Sharing it has, at times, felt like baring my soul, but if readers can relate to even seconds of the experiences, then the vulnerability will not be in vain.

In addressing the question of my network, I've mentally tried to take myself back to networking situations. In them, I am not the guy who chats with strangers in the elevator or blankets a cocktail party with business cards. I've realized that I have zero interest in what most people think of as networking. Have I built a substantial network of valuable relationships with a wide variety of people? Yes. I just didn't do it in a traditional way. I did it by knowingly and unknowingly investing in being the best version of myself. That can mean a lot of different things, but the underlying theme is about sacrifice in the name of self-improvement. It is about asking yourself "Am I closer to my mission and core principles this month than I was last month?" and being able to answer with an unequivocal "yes." Being the best version of myself has attracted — rather than built — my network.

In that spirit, 80 percent of this chapter examines what the process of self-improvement has looked like and continues to look like for me. The remaining 20 percent covers rules of thumb about tightening relationships with those who've been attracted to my network because the 80 percent is getting the attention it needs. I stick to that ratio.

The analogy I often make to hammer home the importance of self-improvement is to that of preflight announcements. You've heard them so often that you've learned to tune them out. Especially the most important part—in the case of an emergency, you must first put your own mask on and ensure that oxygen is flowing before you can help someone else. Simply put, you can't help anyone else, if you haven't helped yourself. Similarly, before you build for others, you have to fortify what's within. I learned this the hard way—for most of my professional years, I was thriving through diverse external experiences and financially intriguing opportunities, but internally I was self-destructing. And I vouched never to be in that position again.

Today, when I think about the building blocks of that 80 percent—of the self-improvement that allows me to wake up to a version of JQ that I like every morning, I've distilled it to three categories: my physical health, my mental health, and my circle. These three categories are in no particular order. On most days, they feel more like highly interconnected spaces that bleed into one another instead of being clean-cut building blocks. However, I believe that there is real value in attempting to journey through them as separate and distinct components, because I've experienced the magic of their domino effect—when I've managed to improve one, the other two have often followed.

My Physical Health
Par for the Course
I grew up with an abundance of blessings—unconditional parental love, a home that bustled with the warmth of ex-

tended family, and a father who still remains my role model. Unfortunately, healthy eating habits weren't on that list. My father is from Arkansas, so he never settled for a breakfast shy of a thousand calories. His job as a mortician often had him up early in the mornings, making him the one to get my brothers and me ready for school. He'd fix us three-course breakfasts that filled the house with an irresistible aroma of bacon, leaving me with the impression that this was an everyday norm until well into my twenties.

My mother worked a full-time job at Consumers Energy, often having to drive to Bay City and Saginaw, Michigan, each city an hour away, my entire childhood. My granny, Lizzie, would step in to help and watch me after school. She too was from Arkansas, and her cooking was even more authentically Southern than my dad's. On any regular school night, she would whip up what most folks considered a holiday meal—fried pork chops, smoked neck bones, smothered chicken, greens with hog maw, and mashed potatoes with gravy that could only taste that good because of the butter. It didn't help that my aunt owned a soul food restaurant, and whenever it ran out of dessert, my granny came to the rescue with home-baked goods. Her peach cobbler and banana pudding were unmatched and still remain my desserts of choice on the rare occasion that I have a sweet tooth.

In addition to my family's Southern roots, they worked so hard to shield my upbringing from the palpable effects of deindustrialization and disinvestment that swept through Flint in the 1980s. Teaching me to avoid entanglement in the city's violent crime and to understand that my future was too bright for it took priority; health consciousness never stood a fighting chance. My family dictated what and when I ate—and that was what and when everyone else was eating. Being naturally athletic and on the skinnier side, I managed to be faster and stronger than most of my peers, which also did nothing to force my awareness of physical health.

My FAMU experience didn't encourage anything different. The time I spent with Ade simply began my exposure to a different way of eating, but it didn't necessarily change my eating habits. For each taste of Ade's jollof rice, or the organic foods that I sampled while studying abroad in South Africa, there were many more instances of late-night partying that ended with Tallahassee comfort fast food and early morning hangovers. I can still taste the alcohol-infused fruit inside what we called alpha juice—my fraternity chapter's party mixture.

I subsequently left college and immersed myself in my work with Tavis Smiley. Tavis was a relentless grinder, forcing everyone who worked for him into the same space. My responsibilities for him required a ton of travel, a setup that didn't lend itself to coming up a steep health consciousness learning curve. I was based in Washington, DC, but spent so little time there that my most vivid memories of the city are social. To this day, I know more about how and where to procure DC late-night food than anyone else. What can I say? Old habits die hard.

I returned to Michigan to join Mayor Kilpatrick's team at the ripe age of twenty-four. I was under the impression that nothing was going to be quite as high paced as my travel for Tavis, but I was mistaken. Kilpatrick's intensity quickly disincentivized anyone on our team from skipping a beat. There was simply too much to do for the city of Detroit and its citizens. I fell right back into the work-hard, play-hard routine that felt familiar. Playing hard entailed a daily engagement with Detroit's nightlife that I'd been away from for over six years. I have zero social regrets about this period in my life but on a health consciousness yardstick, it measured abysmally.

A Rude Awakening

My first wake-up call about my physical health came at the age of twenty-six. I made my way to a casual check-up, the first I recall since college graduation. Dr. Smitherman drew a regular blood panel, after which we parted ways, neither of us making anything of the interaction. I was young, handsome, and felt invincible. Doctor appointments were low on my pyramid of responsibilities.

Dr. Smitherman personally called me several days later. In an alarming voice, he urged me to return to his office to discuss my bloodwork. I might have been slightly nervous but felt largely unencumbered by the phone call and went about my day. For better or worse, it's hard to be concerned without being aware—the two are like closely associated cousins. I went back to the doctor's office the day after his phone call. As I sat down across from him, his large desk between us, I could feel the heavy weight of his concern in the air of that room before he even opened his mouth.

He slid my bloodwork results across the desk with a red pen circling a line item called LDL. I haven't forgotten the number next to it. It read 202. Without the prolific and pervasive use of the internet that we are accustomed to today, I blankly stared at the piece of paper. I had no idea what LDL or that number meant. Dr. Smitherman quickly read my confusion and went on to explain that LDL, or low-density lipoproteins, is a measure of bad cholesterol. He compared my cholesterol to that of a sixty-year-old man. He went on to explain that I was at major risk of having a stroke or a heart attack. He painted a gruesome picture of how my life could unfold if I didn't get my diet under control. He gave me a handful of tips—cut back on fried foods to one meal a month, lessen my intake of dairy products, eat oatmeal every morning, and exercise three times a week. We agreed that I'd come back for a blood test three months later.

I left the appointment alarmed, scared, and confused. At twenty-six years old, my interaction with that doctor marked the first time that anyone spoke to me about health consciousness with intention. Let that sink in and appreciate how much undoing and reconditioning upon which I was about to embark. I didn't necessarily have the vocabulary at the time, but before I could cut my fried food consumption to once a month, I had to understand my why.

What were my triggers? What was putting me in the situation to have fried food on almost a daily basis? I quickly figured out that alcohol was my initial trigger. It often led to partying bigger and longer, which culminated in fast food at either the end of the night or the following morning. I've relied on the thought process of tracking down and analyzing my why many times after that moment. Especially when I've wanted to make a change.

An Uphill Battle

Even after I isolated my why, it still often felt easier said than done. Begrudgingly, I had to cut out of many social situations earlier than usual. I had to turn down a lot of party invitations as I literally worked to rewire the neural pathways about health consciousness in my brain. I was trekking uphill, feet weighed down by years of poor habit formation, fighting to lower that LDL number in my bloodwork for three months. It wasn't easy and there were regressions, but I tried to ground myself. I would think about my father, who quit drinking and smoking, cold turkey, in his early thirties at my mom's relentless urging. Growing up, he continuously told me that we shared a similar sense of willpower—I finally understood what he meant during this time.

Three months later, my LDL number dropped to somewhere between 160 and 170. I can see that my doctor was impressed, and I breathed a major sigh of relief. The number was still high by medical standards, but I felt like I turned a major corner and understood how to lower it further. With all that said, my focus on lowering it still left me on the defensive side of this battle—I was hedging against a really frightening downside.

Force of Nature through the Birth of My Children
I didn't find myself on the offensive side of this physical health challenge until I had children. Children who came into this world with a clean slate about health consciousness and had nothing but upside. In the first few months of my oldest kid's life, I had two stark realizations. The first was that she was watching me and that, even during the initial days of her life, she was taking notes. If I wanted her to gravitate toward vegetables for dinner, I had to model the behavior and actually enjoy it. The second was a paradigm shift about responsibility. I was no longer responsible for just

myself; I was also responsible for her. That meant making decisions that left me with enough mental and physical energy to be present for the task of fatherhood and that protected her.

Not having to focus on lowering my LDL stats gave me significantly more latitude for trial and error. After being accustomed to a heavy meat diet my entire life, I experimented with plant-based foods that were known for their immune system-boosting and detoxing qualities. Admittedly, I had a hard time feeling full after just a salad at first, but I quickly realized that drinking a lot of water got the job done. Now, you'll rarely catch me in my office without a refillable water bottle, also my Zoom conference call staple.

Additionally, I experimented with vitamins and supplements, incorporating these into my daughters' lives from the onset, while incorporating them into mine in parallel. To this day, I get clowned for the number of supplements in my suitcase, but given my professional travel demands, I can't risk contracting an illness and taking it home to my kids. As such, I fortify my nutritional intake in a way that leaves little to chance.

Interestingly enough, the past five years have witnessed explosive growth in nutritional psychiatry, a field that explores the consequences and correlations between what we eat, how we feel, and how we ultimately behave and the kinds of bacteria that live in our guts.

Serotonin is a neurotransmitter that helps regulate sleep and appetite, mediate moods, and inhibit pain. Because 95 percent of serotonin is produced in the gastrointestinal tract, and that tract is lined with a hundred million neurons, it makes sense that the inner workings of our digestive system don't just help us digest food—they guide our emotions. What's more, the function of these neurons and the production of neurotransmitters, like serotonin, is highly influenced by the billions of good bacteria that make up our intestinal microbiome. These bacteria can go from good to bad quickly, if we ingest copious amounts of fried and processed foods, thus negatively affecting our moods.

I was pleased to stumble on this research because it gave my health consciousness transformation an academic voice. While the transformation started out of necessity, I can fully attest to its psychological benefits, especially once I found myself on the offensive. These findings also bring the importance of diet full circle because they translate into a logic that says, "The better you eat, the better you feel about yourself." Let me complete that logic by saying, "The better you feel about yourself, the more folks gravitate toward an authentic version of you." Relationships begin to go from being party-based to being soul-based and those are the relationships that define a network.

In closing out my reflections on physical health, I want to underscore three key thoughts.

1. It was not easy. Confronting a life-threatening reality at twenty-six years old and figuring out how to correct it was an exercise in resourcefulness and strength of mind. There were lots of lows. I still have to fight the urge to have those Cheetos. People need to accept this and learn to forgive themselves. It saves a lot of heartache later.

2. Change typically catalyzes in one of two ways—the downside is heart-wrenchingly painful, or the upside is boundlessly fruitful. Prospect theory dictates that losses are a bigger motivator than gains. I agree, but only when it comes to sparking initial change. Fear of loss doesn't sustain change for the long haul. Focusing on the upside does. Make sure to play the long game.

3. Journey through the mental steps of finding a personal why, be it about good or bad behavior. Focus on manipulating it intently to change that behavior. Presenting the best version of self becomes meaningfully harder if individuals can't connect to their deepest motivations.

My Mental Health
Questions and Explorations
Like many African American families around the US in the 1980s, my family had an intimate relationship with

Christianity and with the black church. My father is heavily involved in First Trinity Missionary Baptist Church, in Flint, Michigan, to this day. My parents relied on the church for uplifting social interactions and viewed it as a safe space to escape the mental pressures of raising a family in a quickly deindustrializing city. The church gave my parents an illusion of mental peace.

I obliged them in my Sunday attendance but was always a curious kid. From a fairly young age, I asked myself and my family subversive questions about concepts that simply never made sense. I couldn't wrap my mind around why images of a white God were plastered all over a black church. I didn't agree with the folks who draped themselves in dapper outfits to "cleanse their souls" on Sundays, only to be seen doing illicit things in the neighborhood as soon as they stepped foot outside the church.

Coming into my own as a young man, I had a hard time reconciling the church's rhetoric about sexuality. Family conversations about these topics would quickly hit a dead end. Not because my parents didn't want to entertain the unconventional thoughts of their youngest child, but because they didn't necessarily have the tools to do so. After leaving the house for college, I quickly shed any guilt I had over not incorporating church into my independent life. Well over a decade passed before I was meaningfully able to explore this area of my life.

In late 2015, I traveled to Israel with a group of leaders from the Midwest. I can't say that I was jumping up and down to go on the trip, or that I knew much about Israel, but I did like to travel. The organizers of the trip sought to educate our group on the importance of the US–Israel relationship and about Israel's contributions to the world. As soon as I told my friends that I opted to go on the trip, I was bombarded with comments and questions—"Stay safe. The conflict is real."—along with many permutations thereof. While the trip did open my eyes to the intricacies of the conflict and of life in a seventy-year-old nation, it did far more to reawaken my longstanding questions about religion, especially during our time in Jerusalem.

Touring Jerusalem felt like traveling in a time machine. The gravity and magnitude of history was palpable as I walked on cobblestones laid down over three thousand years ago. The mixing of Judaism, Christianity, and Islam in the city was fascinating. I remember entering the Holy Sepulchre, the place where Jesus's body was said to have been between burial and resurrection, and making my way to our tour guide, an archaeologist by training. His storytelling was intriguing, but it led me to ask a slew of questions as I struggled to connect my biblical insights with his presentation. I persistently asked about what has been proven. His answers chalked up to "surprisingly little." These interactions affirmed my many years of discomfort with Christianity and with the black church.

The process of unpacking what happened in Israel only began when I returned to the United States. It took several months before I was able to formulate my own plan for exploring religions outside of Christianity. In June 2016, I started that process. I decided to dedicate a year to learning about the top twelve religions, focusing on one each month. In addition to reading books, perusing the internet, and talking to knowledgeable parties, I was going to have as many immersive experiences of worship in each of the religions as possible.

African Spirituality

I was six months into the journey when I came across a lecture on African spirituality. The suggested links kept appearing on my YouTube and Facebook ads for months before I decided to click through. As the lecture unfolded, I began to feel proverbially at home—much like I felt when I studied abroad in South Africa through FAMU's program. To start, African spirituality has its roots on the continent of Africa and existed there long before the Christian and Islamic colonization of the region. Beyond that, African spirituality doesn't separate itself from aspects of culture, society, or environment. Instead, it is a way of life that links the physical to the spiritual and that paved the way for how we think about holistic living today. For example, sickness in the indigenous African worldview is not only an imbalance in the body, but it is also an imbalance in one's social life, said to be linked to a breakdown in one's kinship and family relations.

Another aspect of African spirituality that resonated with me was its reverence for and incorporation of ancestors. As unusual as it might sound, there have been several occasions when I've tangibly felt my grandmother's presence. I'd hear my granny tell me how proud she is of me, or understand her guiding me to a decision, even though we physically lost her to cancer when I was in the eighth grade. My entire life, I kept these occurrences to myself until African spirituality gave me a framework to understand their meanings.

At its core, African spirituality teaches that we have to align with nature instead of making nature align with us. This flexibility partially stems from the idea that African spiritual beliefs are not bound by the rigidity of a written text. I believe that this flexibility is the reason why these practices have sustained. Nature is always with us no matter how much we fight its flow.

Over the years, I've felt the mental and physical discomfort of being "against the flow." I've also been able to pick up on the energy and vibration of other people in an acute sense of the word. I've known that despite the number of people I interact with, few people's energy elevates, or even compliments, my own. Before I encountered African mindfulness on my journey of religious exploration, I didn't have the tools or the vocabulary to articulate these feelings. Instead, they sat in an uncomfortable purgatory of unprocessed thoughts. Now, I am able to lean on them for personal and professional decision-making.

Meditation

An even more tangible practice that African spirituality has brought into my life is meditation. As I've made my way down the road of an entrepreneur, I've felt lonely and overwhelmed. Life in the fast lane isn't an experience that many folks can relate to directly. On a daily basis, I am running three businesses and fathering my kids intentionally. This comes with stressors that I can only describe as a strong wedge between the body and the soul. While my discovery of transcendental meditation can occupy an entire chapter by itself, it's at the core of what has helped me get my mind and my body to be of one accord.

I first encountered meditation while attempting yoga to decompress. The most enjoyable part of yoga wasn't the poses, but rather the breathing techniques that quieted my mind, even for a few seconds. Soon enough, I started trying the breathing techniques on my own, away from yoga classes, in my own home or in the serene park by the lake in my neighborhood. I never knew how loud my mind could be until I tried to quiet it. Conquering even two successful minutes of meditation took me months.

The more I steeped myself in this practice, the more I began to understand the concept of chakra, a circular vortex of energy in the body that is opened through yoga and/or meditation. Chakras take in, incorporate, and emanate energy that keeps people functioning at optimal levels. Today, nearly three years after I began to practice meditation, I wear three bracelets on a daily basis—one with a tiger eye, a crystal that holds the vibration of source, known for being a conduit of purpose; one with stones for each of the seven chakras; and one with stones for harmony and peace. They serve as a constant reminder of what I've coined as "being in the flow"—of following my intuition and the guidance of my African ancestors back to the people and places that align with my spirit.

Visualization

When folks who haven't had the exposure ask about what meditation feels like, I explain it as a resyncing of sorts, a recalibration achieved through separating from social media, from friends, from family, and from work—it is an intentional, uninterrupted submersion in nature. It's about sitting still and letting nothingness drown out everything else in the mind. It has been a lifesaver and a lever of control, especially on days where it feels like I'm not in the flow. Not only has it helped me re-center, it has also allowed me to make space for the kind of visualization that enables dreaming big.

Not everyone appreciates American entrepreneur Dame Dash, best known for cofounding Roc-A-Fella Records with Jay-Z and Kareem Burke, the way I do. But in discussing visualization, I can't help but quote one of his Instagram posts. In an interview on May 21, he said the following:

> If I want something, I go into the future in my brain, which is powerful, and I visualize exactly what I want. So I am there, I am in my future—like I was just in the future thinking about watching myself on my television network. So because I do that, that means I have to think about what would be the worst-case scenario. Then I have to think about what would be the best-case scenario. Then I eliminate every single thing that I think could happen, which I call architecting. Then I put everything in—every single attitude, and person around me in my vision that's going to make me get to what I want.

This resonates because I've leaned on the power of visualization as early as my high school years, when I envisioned that I'd be working with Tavis Smiley and left no stone unturned to accomplish it. I've also deployed it in the context of relationship building. Often, I've wanted to connect with or get close to someone but really didn't know how it would happen. In the spirit of Dame Dash's words, I would direct a lot of mental energy simply thinking about a future scenario in which it did happen, and, in a majority of cases, it actually would.

Visualization is an unstoppable tool, but the reality is that people have to have the mental space and peace to do it. It's incredibly difficult to dedicate energy to visualizing something if the mind is running in circles at a million miles an hour. Meditation has come to the rescue time and time again in helping me free my mental space to focus on the things that advance me, rather than on those that deter, aggravate, or are out of my control. The appendix of this book offers simplified, tangible, steps that people can follow to near a meditative state. I've also offered tunes that I've found to be effective as I've made my own way through the practice of meditation.

Therapy

As accretive as the teachings of African spirituality have been to my mental health, there have honestly been times where I've felt like I just can't do it alone. Friends are great and so is meditation, but sometimes people need a trained professional. COVID-19 has been a perfect storm of personal and professional circumstances that have evoked an anxiety that I am not used to. Quarantine has mitigated my typical stress outlets and tampered with access to my preferred spaces of reprieve. In moments like these, I am an unequivocal proponent of cognitive therapy.

As a man of color, I grew up with the same stigma about resorting to therapy as is painfully familiar to many others who look like me. "You're weak," people would say in our communities. "That's some bullshit," they would comment on the corners of our neighborhoods. It goes without saying that it's also an expensive endeavor. But I am glad to see that, individual by individual, we are moving beyond this mindset and choosing to prioritize it in our spending.

To my readers of color—I know that I don't need to explain the role that trauma has played in shaping who we are. To all my readers—let me highlight that these direct and indirect experiences of trauma are real, and they weigh on you, chipping away at your psyche, at your ability to be vulnerable and to build close relationships if they're not dealt with. Your friends and your families love you, but they aren't objective, and they aren't trained. Let's get a trained professional with letters behind their name involved. If it is a person of color—even better.

Collectively, our communities need a tremendous amount of healing. Need we look further than the daily news cycle of 2020? Whether disproportionately decimated by a pandemic or by white cops on the street, we are faced with constant reminders that we haven't leveled the playing field for basic civil liberties. We aren't immune to the daily struggles of dysfunctional relationships, difficult work situations, and financial struggles either, so we can quickly find ourselves in an emotional pressure cooker. And while diamonds are created under pressure, we actually have to retain our sanity to reap the benefits of our diamonds. It is crucial to protect our mental peace, because, just like our time, it is damn near impossible to replenish once it is gone.

My Circle
Zeke and Berton

Two weeks before I wrote this section of my book, I got a call from Berton, a friend and a brother who has been there for the ups and downs. I didn't know what Berton was going to say when I picked up, mostly because I never know what Berton is going to say. His explosive energy and un-aberrated honesty always have a way of keeping me on my toes. I picked up the phone and Berton notified me that he and Isaiah, also known as Zeke in our circle, are coming to Detroit to link up. "We know you need it, man," he said. It was true. I did need it, as I stood in the eye of a perfect storm of unprecedented personal and professional challenges.

In the heart of Michigan's COVID-19 stay-at-home order, Berton, Zeke, and I found ourselves socially distancing in the open air of Belle Isle, a multi-acre park in Detroit. I plead the fifth on whether we were allowed to be there, not that Berton would've cared anyway. He's rarely deterred and was so determined to lend his support that he barely gave Zeke an explanation for why he had to be in his ride making the drive from Flint to Detroit on an hour's notice. I wasn't surprised that Zeke didn't ask too many questions—our circle has a deeply rooted trust in one another's intuition.

The next two hours were soul-healing in a way that I didn't even know I needed, and that is only created through true brotherhood. We covered it all—the good, the bad, and the ugly, and we switched among the three seamlessly. In a matter of hours, we vacillated between being on the verge of tears and laughing so uncontrollably that there was no doubt that the three of us speak the same proverbial language.

In the days that followed, I did a lot of thinking about the way that our circle is set up. What does it take for my circle to see me through my good, my bad, and my ugly?

With conviction, I can say what it doesn't take. It doesn't take some arbitrarily long period of time. As people, we have an understandable tendency to correlate the closeness of relationships with the amount of time passed since their inception. It's not to say that time isn't important at all, but time isn't the only factor. Far too often we allow ourselves to be dragged down by longstanding relationships that no longer feed us. I can think of a few instances, with both family and friends, in which time spotlighted a divergence in values, helping me realize that despite fond memories, a person no longer belonged in my small, intimate inner circle.

As such, my close-knit friendship with Zeke and Berton has only crystallized over the past two to three years. With a limited amount of free time and a high number of demands on it, all three of us would agree that we weren't necessarily looking for new friends or sources of camaraderie. But like the best kind of love, as Zeke would say, sometimes it shows up at the doorstep and it can't be ignored. It is important for high-performing individuals to know when to let go and when something worth paying attention to is at the doorstep.

Berton showed up at my doorstep when we accidentally ran into each other at the NAACP National Convention in Philadelphia. I hadn't seen him in at least four years. My memories of him were from attending karate class as kids growing up in Flint, but catching up in Philadelphia felt like no time had passed. An instant alignment in our energies allowed us to create the kind of safe space that Zeke will say isn't even replicable with family. Berton shared that he was in the midst of a professional transition, making his way out of a job to focus on figuring out just what he wanted to do next. I was no stranger to transitions as I had grappled with whether to move back to Michigan for Mayor Kilpatrick, and later with whether to leave corporate America.

When we got back, Berton and I committed to a weekly brother's breakfast club. We used these breakfasts to discuss how to capitalize on our relationships and talents and to push each other to do more in our communities, especially the black community. At the time, I had no idea that Berton and I would end up working together professionally. I simply related to the transition he was facing and thought I could be a sounding board. He didn't articulate the deep impact that our conversations had on his trajectory until recently. This solidified what I had long known—true brotherhood isn't transactional, and it's built long before we need to lean on it.

Zeke and I connected over his leadership journey. The nonprofit professional space he works in is an interesting phenomenon because it's full of bleeding hearts who can be scared to run the show like a business, and who often want to blur the personal-professional lines. Zeke was looking to grow in his effectiveness as a leader without getting involved in what happens when the personal-professional divide is crossed. This was something I understood deeply, and a skill that I've long been practicing.

Over time, I've worked on an increasing number of projects with a social impact component through The BTL Group. Each and every time, I've pushed against the natural impetus to get emotionally attached to the relationships involved. It amuses me when Zeke says that this ability is one of my greatest strengths, because I've struggled with it as much as he does. I simply laser focused on it early in life. Consulting is a relationship business, and it's hard to operate objectively if there is an emotional attachment to the relationships.

Bringing Zeke, Berton, and me together, there is a spectrum of demeanors, and I wouldn't want it any other way. Zeke describes himself as the more logic-driven, conservative one who indulges in having as many answers up front as possible. Berton is our out-of-the-box friend. He has an unconventional relationship with boundaries and basically does whatever he wants. We'll ask Berton to execute something seemingly complicated, and he'll call it "light work." We won't know how, but it'll be done immediately. I walk a line somewhere in the middle. Zeke would probably say that I'm grounded, and that I game plan, but only to a point. Ultimately, I am the maverick of our group—unafraid to go down the path less traveled, especially if it's after something that I want badly enough.

Our dynamic exists in an ecosystem of the essentials—mutual trust, respect, and understanding—that we probably take somewhat for granted, but the importance of which can't be overstated. If a relationship doesn't have that, it'll be hard to have much else. Having the essentials enables us to compensate for one another's weaknesses, and amplify one another's strengths, rendering whatever we put our collective minds to. Berton says that there's no such thing as weakness when we are together—we're perfect in our imperfections. In considering the role that Zeke and Berton have played in the past few years of my life, I feel honestly blessed to be the "average" one. I believe that if individuals are not the average ones of the three to five people they consider the closest, they're hardly growing.

Closeness isn't always an easy thing. Closeness means actively listening to dissenting opinions. It means internalizing when your brother or your sister has looked you in the eye and called you out on f*cking up. It means treating your friends like family, not just when they agree with you, but also when they don't. Solid conflict resolution sits at the heart of that, and I thought that it was important to touch on the topic, even though Zeke, Berton, and I have barely had to engage in any.

Zeke's most recent description of conflict resolution was better than any other that I've heard, so I figured that there was no need to recreate the wheel. He likened it to a video game series called *Sonic the Hedgehog*. In it, the protagonist moves through the game's universe, picking up coins. As he navigates his path, he runs into spikes, which cause him to lose coins. The goal is to finish the game coin positive, because if the coins run out before the game does, the protagonist dies.

Much like the game, you accumulate coins in relationships as you build, as you share in meaningful experiences, as you show up for one another, and as you work together successfully. Think of it as depositing into an emotional bank account. When there is serious friction that can't be brushed off or fixed with a conversation, you hit a spike, or you lose coins; you withdraw from the emotional bank account. The goal is to keep your closest relationships coin positive by accumulating more coins than you lose so that you have a buffer in the difficult times.

Jason

Whereas I think about Zeke and Berton as peers, Jason plays the role of an older brother. Jason is seven years older— seven years that are saturated with life experiences and a wisdom that leaves me with food for thought every time we connect. Jason lost his wife to cancer last year. As I've tried to be there for him, I've been inspired by his strength, reflections, and sense of perspective.

Given how particular I am with allowing folks into my life, the fact that Jason is named as the executor on my will tells you a lot about how much I trust his judgment. Along the same lines, Jason is the godfather of one of my daughters, another space that I protect fearlessly. He is also a meaningful part of my memories with the late social capital expert Marlowe Stoudemire, a dear friend taken too soon by COVID-19. In an unspoken way, Jason and I feel inextricably linked in the continuation of Marlowe's legacy of community activism, mentorship, and relentless optimism about the future of Detroit and the world.

Zeke, Berton, and Jason—that's an intentionally small number of fellas. Intentionally small because when it comes to your circle, choose quality over quantity. Choose to play the long relationship-building game over the one of immediate gratification. Choose folks who you aspire to be like over those who are simply content with the status quo. Don't understate the importance of your support system in the rigorous self-improvement process that I call on you to invest in.

The Remaining 20 Percent

I promised that I'd spend some time discussing how I approach fortifying the relationships that I already have. It might not be the feedback that you're expecting, but the approach lies in focusing on the process. The human need for answers or for the final analysis is a strong one, and it pushes us to expedite the motions of actually getting to know someone. But I've found more satisfaction in slowing down and actually asking the right questions—in letting the questions hold the answers. This might feel like it stands in contradiction to my assertion about how time isn't a super important factor in relationships, but it doesn't.

Each relationship has a cadence of its own—a flow. The goal is to not expedite the natural flow, but rather to use it as an opportunity to listen actively and to understand someone's underlying motivation. This is an exercise in undeniable patience. Sometimes I also want to cut corners—it's only human. But then I consider the power of letting someone reveal himself or herself on their own terms and giving that someone the space to do so. You rarely ever get it wrong when you let the cards unfold organically without focusing on the outcome.

As I wrap up what I view as the most personal chapter of this book, I can't help but think about the Cheetos that I indulged in at ten P.M. last night, the dysfunctional interactions that I want to take back, and the phone calls that I haven't necessarily returned to all the folks who I want to speak with. All of that is to say that what I've spelled out continues to challenge me. On some days, it prompts me to ask more questions than I can answer. But, on some days, the future feels so bright because the work of self-improvement is the most worthwhile work of all.

From: Afoggy@   - Block Sender
To: jquar   Save Address
CC: tsmiley@   Save Address
Subject: **Conditions**
Date: Thu, 27 Jul 2000 20:06:33 EDT
Reply   Reply All   Forward   Delete   Previous   Next   Close

Dear Jonathan:

I am happy to inform you that the Tavis Smiley Foundation will sponsor you to attend the Advocacy in the Next Millenium symposium on August 12th. You made a great impression on Tavis Smiley and his staff during the Detroit Youth to Leaders conference. We want to help you reach your goals and develop your leadership skills.

These are the following conditions that you must agree to in order for sponsorship to attend the Advocacy in the Next Millenium symposium in Los Angeles, California.

1) You and your parents must sign a release form stating that Tavis Smiley Foundation and Tavis Smiley will not be held a liable.

2) Please do not discuss anything related to your sponsorship and the Advocacy in the Millenium to anyone outside your immediate family and media contacts until after the event. We are only providing one sponsorship - and you are it.

3) You will be responsible for contacting and securing articles in at least three of the following: the Black Teen Enterprise Magazine, a local newspaper, The Source, NNPA (Black Newspapers Association), Vibe, Honey, XXL or any other publications that have a young black audience.

4) You will have an adult escort, Raymond Ross, (he travels with Tavis) for the entirety of your trip.

The Tavis Smiley Foundation will arrange for you to be picked up and dropped off from the airport. Your meals will be covered for Friday night and Saturday all day. Attached is an agreement for your parents. Please return the contract and contact me no later than Monday, July 31st. I need to get your ticket off before I leave on Wednesday for Philadelphia.

Your flight has been reserved for Aug 11 leaving Detroit at 7:30 a.m. with a connection in Chicago and arriving in Long Beach at 11:12 a.m. You will leave Sunday, Aug 13 at 6:55 a.m. from Long Beach, connect through Dallas and arrive in Detroit at 4:36 a.m. Please note that these are the only flight accomodations that will be provided - this is a restricted ticket. So please let me know if you have any schedule conflicts. All your time will be with Raymond Ross or the Tavis Smiley Foundation Staff. Please forward your home phone number.

Email invitation to attend Tavis Smiley's
State of the Black Union, *2000*

Me, State of the Black Union; Los Angeles, CA, *2000*

Bill Quarles, dad
(in his office at Greene Home for Funerals), *1988*

Ruthy Quarles, mom; Jeremiah Quarles, brother, *1983*

Lizzie Mae Wilbon, grandmother, *1985*

Tavis Smiley, boss & mentor
Reception for Youth Leader of the Year Award
Los Angeles, *2001*

Ingrid Saunders-Jones
Chairwoman of Coca-Cola Foundation & Mentor
Summer Internship as Coca-Cola Scholar, *2001*

L to R: Bella Quarles, Emerson Quarles, Jai Quarles, daughters, *2017*

Chapter 5
Beyond the Here and Now

We don't plan to fail, but we fail to plan.
—Jonathan Quarles

Over the past several years, I've done a lot of thinking about legacy. What does it actually mean to build something that lives far beyond the here and now? The existence of my kids has definitely evoked some of this introspection but that isn't the complete picture. Many of these reflections have been intimately connected to a ubiquitous sense of gratitude for my blessings and to a deeply seated drive to make them count in a real way.

As I was in the flow of building what felt right at various stages of my professional years, I wasn't fully conscious of how influential a forward-looking mindset was to the process. I was lucky enough to have a father who constantly stressed the tactical importance of planning ahead and that is sort of where it ended.

Today, I am more in touch with the metaphysical nature of success and legacy. The universe is almost entirely mental. Let that sink in for a moment. If we direct our mental energy toward conceptualizing something that will last forever, we begin to go through the motions of building it that way. If we're building sustainably, it will sustain. In both instances, the end result is more likely to be something that stands the test of time.

I can't take the mental step of conceptualization for you, but I can give you the "cheat cards"—the simple, but important, ideas that often get overlooked, especially by black entrepreneurs and changemakers. When it comes to sustainability, I view wealth planning, mentorship, and effective community organizing as the tactical cheat cards. Beyond that, it is my hope that the food for thought in this chapter will be a call to action—whatever you're building in the personal, professional, and communal domains, build to make it last.

Wealth Planning
Professional Advice
Most folks I've encountered, even those from notoriously wealthy communities, miss the mark on wealth planning. Wealth planning isn't something to initiate when you've made the money. This rings particularly true in 2020, when technology companies quadruple in value overnight. Even if we weren't living in an age of artificially inflated valuations, wealth accumulation is a fundamentally forward-looking exercise that usually benefits from the passage of time. It is also a multi-pronged endeavor with tentacles in several underlying concepts. My goal isn't to turn this into a wealth planning manual. Rather, it is to give you foundational ideas to consider.

I'll begin with the concept of hiring help. Hiring help but remaining an active participant in your wealth-planning process is essential. I am a staunch believer that, just as with therapy, there are some things that we shouldn't be doing by ourselves because the stakes are too high. Wealth planning is one of those. There is a misconception that you need a lot of money to partner with a financial advisor—however, that thinking is flawed. Off the top of my head, I can think of a few up-and-coming advisors who understand and value the concept of growing with their clients. Financial advisors are also more likely to help you, regardless of your net worth, if you have a big network, because they will see the partnership as a marketing play for themselves. I advise all those interested to scope out an advisor within five years of college graduation.

The next natural question is about how to approach that process. I view it as an optimization of your comfort and the advisor's expertise. I believe that advisor selection is 60 percent comfort and 40 percent expertise, unless you have a highly esoteric personal financial situation. Remember, advisors are overseeing an important and personal space in your life, and if they're going to be effective, they need to be able to converse with you freely.

I give expertise an intentionally lower weighting because financial advice is commoditized for the most part—no one is winning meaningful market share on exceptional performance. It's more about understanding how to capitalize on existing trends in the market, than it is about beating it by a large percentage over a long period of time. As a result, there should definitely be a strategy with measurable benchmarks that are proper reflections of your income-producing abilities, goals, and risk tolerance.

I think about my own financial landscape in several logical buckets: long-term, mid-term, and short-term. The short-term bucket is always focused on investments that have a liquid market and can be easily turned into cash. Outside of these, I have a rainy-day fund, and the amount in it fluctuates between three and six months of basic expenses, depending on circumstances.

As with friends, not all advisors suit you at all stages and levels of your own evolution. Don't allow your sense of loyalty to get the best of you and cause you to hold onto a professional you have outgrown. I've had to change my advisor in the past few years, after recognizing that my former advisor was simply going through the motions, as opposed to partnering with me to strategize for the future.

I'll close my perspective on advisors with the same concept that I opened with, which is that the process of wealth planning and accumulation requires your active involvement. At the end of the day, no one will look out for you in the way that you will look out for yourself. Don't leave your assets solely in the hands of someone else. Be resourceful, ask questions, and read the research reports to develop a personal conviction in how your money is being handled. Aim for a level of understanding such that you can explain how your money is being invested to another person. In addition, always monitor the returns. I recommend that you do it regularly, but not every day. The day-to-day volatility of personal portfolios can distract you from staying focused on the long game.

Takeaway: Hire a financial advisor (aim to do it within five years of college graduation) but continue to remain an active participant in your wealth building, planning, and maintenance.

The Credit Game

Understanding credit is an indispensable piece of playing the long game of wealth building. I find that attitudes toward credit typically live on two extremes. One camp is fearful and avoids credit like the plague. The other overindulges and spends on credit as if the money is owned, not owed. I believe that the most effective attitude is somewhere in the middle. As I began to interact with credit, I found myself in the former camp. I remember getting my first credit card in college—it had no more than a $500 credit limit. I would allow myself to purchase two items with it every month and pay the bill immediately. Sitting where I am today, this feels more like comic relief than good habit development.

However, I believe that those teachable moments were critical in helping me develop a healthy relationship with credit. That relationship began with exposure. It's easy to fear or avoid something that you don't interact with. I look forward to the day that my kids are old enough to have work permits because that will also be the day they receive their first credit cards. When it comes to building a solid credit score, time matters. The longer you're interacting with credit, the better. Even if your credit limits and balances are low, time still matters.

I would argue that indulgent attitudes toward credit can be nipped in the bud with early exposure. Credit damage is fairly limited with first-time credit card holders because the credit limit is typically low. Additionally, if you overspend in your early years, there is plenty of time to correct the damage to your credit score. That is more challenging as time goes on because each incremental positive action has less impact.

As a black business owner, it becomes increasingly more important to ensure that you learn and understand how to play the credit game. People of color struggle with access to all kinds of credit. Compound that with a poor credit score, and your hands are entirely tied. While I am not a fan of taking on unnecessary debt, sometimes the math is clear. In a financial sense of the word, not only is debt cheaper than equity, but debt can also help compound returns, depending on the circumstances. I view debt as one of the many tools in a business development arsenal, and my goal has always been to expand my options before I need to resort to them.

My final note of caution on credit echoes my thinking on wealth building, which is about active participation. Given that credit is not taught in either the public or private school systems, almost everyone has had to learn to read the fine print the hard way. So yes, read the fine print before you sign on the dotted line. Know your interest rate. Seek to understand both the fee and the benefit profiles of your credit cards. Like many other vehicles for growth and sustainability, credit can be a blessing and a curse. A forward-looking mindset will help you have more instances of the former.

Takeaway: Your credit score has several inputs, but time is an important one. Start building your relationship with credit as soon as possible; it gives you more room to fix the blunders.

The Tax Game

Even more than credit, having a good tax strategy is akin to playing a game of poker with a stack of cards fixed in your favor. There is a lot to say on effective tax planning, but I want to offer a creative beginning step that most folks overlook—form an LLC and make yourself the owner and managing member. It doesn't matter whether you plan to offer services or conduct commerce, LLCs are powerful platforms for lowering taxable income.

While we might not be thinking along these lines, we are constantly engaging in activities that can be written off as business or professional development items, given the presence of a self-owned business. These activities run the gamut from the mundane, like allocating a portion of your internet and phone usage to the development of your LLC, to the more exciting, like your travel adventures with an educational component. One by one, these items add up to move the needle on how much you're paying Uncle Sam.

In case this isn't obvious, let me be clear. This isn't about crossing any legal lines. This is about knowing the system and making it work for you. This is about partnering with an accountant who knows the nooks and crannies and how to use them to your benefit. Just as I argued the benefits of a financial advisor, I am an advocate of hiring someone who will strategize with you, instead of simply filing your taxes. I recently stopped working with a tax service provider whose price tag wasn't commensurate with his value added. This is my first filing season with a newly chosen company, and it's made a world of difference. I have more peace of mind knowing that I am in good hands, though I continue to pay careful attention.

The connection between building wealth and lowering your tax basis is obvious, but the connection between investing and lowering your tax basis might not be. There are interesting ways to save on taxes across almost any asset class—the key lies in having the information. Because this information is neither given to us by family nor taught to us in schools, I reiterate my case for hiring quality professional assistance.

Takeaway: Forming an LLC is an effective way of playing the tax game. Partner with a tax advisor that can teach you the game and help you optimize your tax outcomes.

Business Ownership and Building Equity

It's impossible to deny the painful history that the black community has had with business ownership. It is no surprise that, after centuries of being legislatively and societally locked out of a variety of networks, access to capital, and skill-building opportunities for business ownership, the number of black-owned businesses in the US is painfully small. Because business ownership and inheritance is a major engine of generational wealth, it is also no surprise that the black community is lagging far behind many others in that metric.

From an early age, my father oriented me toward not having a boss. After working so hard to provide for our family, no matter the circumstances, I am certain that a part of him was projecting his own unrealized dreams. Over time, I came to understand that owning my own business is part of my core purpose. I've never liked corporate training. I was always too young for my work accolades, which made already insecure colleagues feel more insecure. Additionally, I've always valued flexibility too much to have a boss in perpetuity. My father identified my independent thinking early on, which is probably why, so many years after we started having those conversations, he noted my entrepreneurial journey as one of his sources of pride in a recently produced video memorializing the stories of the Quarles family.

Business ownership is not for everyone, but I highly recommend trying it at some point, whether you are the founder of a business or purchased it from someone else. Not only is it a microcosm of life—a ride that leaves you with lessons at every turn—but it is also a fundamental driver of wealth creation. The liberty that comes with passing a business down to the carriers of your genes or, at minimum, to whomever you want is unmatched. I can't resist resurfacing Dame Dash when it comes to this topic. In a heated appearance on the Breakfast Club radio show, he articulated the following:

> So you're gonna work twenty years in a business or fifteen years in a business every day. Over and over again, and your son can't work here whenever he feels like it . . . you're clowning me. Can another man tell you you're fired? Yes or no? Can another man say you're

fired? No one can tell me that. That's priceless to me.

The other talking heads on the show imply that they "like getting a check" because they "like the work they do." As he hears this, Dash becomes even more visibly agitated. He claims that this logic is warped because liking the work that you do and getting a paycheck aren't inextricably connected.

You will probably like what you do more if you choose to pursue the idea on your own or if you choose to invest in a majority stake. Every check you pay yourself builds equity in the fruits of your own labor. This isn't something that the world socializes well. The world is more comfortable with breeding a generation of good corporate citizens, but life is more fulfilling when you venture outside the norm.

Something else that I've realized about building equity is that even if you didn't start or buy a business, you can still approach equity creatively. In the earlier days of The BTL Group, I recall having a big data analytics company as my client. Long before big data emerged as the answer to all of the world's problems, I identified it as an important and potent tech trend. Instead of accepting monetary compensation for my services, I asked the company for equity. I continued to do this, managing to build a meaningful position over the course of several months.

Today, the company is exploring a potential sale that I am positioned to gain from. Had the importance of building equity never been on my radar, I wouldn't have dared to ask for pay in that form. If you're not focused on it already, let me be the one who elevates the financial and proverbial value of having equity in whatever you're doing.

Dame Dash's question about whether your son (or daughter) can easily join a business that you've given the vast majority of your life to might sound extreme, but maybe we shouldn't dismiss it as a legitimate consideration. Maybe his question is pointing to what real ownership is all about. In a world where communities of color have so much ground to make up in the realm of business ownership, I'm comfortable having the difficult conversations that will be required to swing the pendulum in the other direction.

History aside, I've viewed business ownership as a rewarding way to be in charge of my fate—to write my own rules, to conjure up my own exit strategies, and to make my own mistakes.

Takeaway: Building ownership and working for your last name, not your first, is rewarding. Seek creative ways to build your equity position in the businesses you believe in. As Black entrepreneurs, this is one of our most potent ways to bend the arc of history.

Your Will and Estate

Confronting mortality is a fundamentally uncomfortable concept, but I've never been all that uncomfortable with it. Maybe it was because I had experienced the loss of several close family members before I was a young adult, but I view confrontation with mortality as an exercise of pragmatism. The only certainties are death and taxes.

My resignation to the realities of mortality has allowed me to handle affairs related to the process at a fairly young age. I would recommend doing the same to anyone else. I am thirty-eight years old at the time of this writing, but I drafted a will dictating the distribution of my assets, the terms of my burial, and a potential text of my obituary several years ago. Not that every second of doing it was enjoyable, but I figured that these are short-term losses for long-term gains.

I don't want the loved ones who will mourn my eventual passing to be encumbered by having to navigate my affairs or to pay tremendous amounts of money for both a burial and a funeral. Instead, I've requested to be cremated, and for the ashes to be distributed to my children. On a more metaphysical level, I've relished the contemplation that drafting a will is inevitably accompanied by.

Whether it's personal, professional, or financial, this book speaks out in defense of exiting situations that no longer work for you. Exiting is one thing, but how you exit is another. I believe that part of leaving a legacy is exiting with the same sense of grace that you entered with. Write that will so you can exit with a level of grace that lives up to the profundity of your life and your legacy.

Takeaway: Will-writing may not be widely discussed, but I highly recommend doing it in your thirties. The process is interestingly cathartic, and you can always make amendments as your life circumstances change. Don't leave this task for the moment you need it and can't do it with a clear mind.

Mentorship
A Misnomer

Today's definition of mentorship is fairly nebulous. Most folks discuss mentors as if they are coaches, confidants, or friends. I think that this paradigm does mentoring relationships a lot of disservice. I would suggest that proper mentorship is not a feel-good sport. It is about creating a lasting legacy. Investing in others is the single most potent way to build beyond the here and now.

The typical mentoring handbook doesn't teach this. It presents a contrived and typically mismatched pairing between someone more junior and someone more senior. Or maybe the pairing happens by circumstance, if we're lucky. The junior person comes to see the senior person on his or her turf every once in a while, so it's "convenient." The pair converses, unintentionally, as the junior person sits with the hope that, at some point in time, the mentor calls in a favor. The mentee looks at this as time well spent. Now, take that handbook and toss it.

Let's reimagine mentorship as the legacy-building tool that it is, and let's discuss what it looks like through that angle. The first thing that I've discovered is that the best mentors are found organically. I remember meeting one of my mentors, Joe, for the first time. It was during my defense lobbying days at Tower Defense & Aerospace. As an outsider coming into the defense industry, I had to make sure that I was in rooms with the decision-makers of that community at all times.

I showed up at one of the Army's networking events and couldn't help but notice the other black male in the room. I spotted his name and took a second to look it up on my iPhone. Quickly, I realized how accomplished Joe was—a West Point Lifetime Achievement Award recipient, Central Michigan University Board of Trustees, Federal Reserve Board of Governors, and that doesn't even begin to cover his accolades. As the night went on, I introduced myself to Joe and had a quick, but authentic, conversation. I got his business card and promised to follow up.

Our first encounter was over drinks. The encounter did not make Joe my mentor; it made him an acquaintance. I didn't just rest on the laurels of familiarity with another man of color. I prepared for our next fifteen encounters as if each of them would be our last. I studied him like it was the bar exam. I read every article, blog, comment, and website to understand who he was and to familiarize myself with his electronic footprint. I digested the information I learned into thoughtful questions based on my life experiences and aspirations for our next encounter. On top of being prepared, I was punctual for every meeting—on time for the creation of an organic mentorship. Even with all the preparation I put in, I didn't see Joe as my mentor until I was able to help him advance his goals.

In his professional life, Joe is the chairman of a holding company that owns and operates several others. One of the businesses he was particularly invested in was stagnating, and he was looking for ways to reignite its growth. Several months into our relationship, I facilitated a partnership between Joe's business and my employer at the time. The partnership allowed Joe's business to test a revolutionizing concept that it believed in. There ended up being a proof of concept, and the business turned the corner on its plateaued growth.

This changed the dynamic of our relationship. Joe began to see me as someone who added value to his personal and professional life, compelling him to invest in me further. This underscores the concept of A players gravitating toward other A players. Solid mentor-mentee relationships are a testament to this concept.

Over the years, I've had many young men reach out to me seeking advice. As someone who genuinely cares about giving back, I lend my time to as many meetings and phone calls as possible. However, I cannot help anyone if they do not help themselves. As a mentee, be authentic. Authenticity is important in every interaction, but especially in the first few encounters. Trying to be anyone other than yourself is hard work, and it can't be sustained for a long period of time. Be prepared. Success is really about opportunity meeting preparation. Folks with extensive life experiences can easily tell the difference between someone who is prepared and someone who is not. Plus, preparation is a high form of respect for someone's time.

Takeaway: Be prepared for all your meetings but definitely for the ones with mentors. Ill-preparedness is very easy to spot, especially with experience.

Capacity Building through Mentorship
Maimonides was a prolific Jewish philosopher of the Middle Ages. His contributions to Jewish thought span many different topics, one of which is charity. Maimonides wrote extensively about how charity can be approached ethically,

111

breaking it down into eight levels. While Maimonides lived close to nine hundred years ago, he viewed capacity building as the highest level of charity. This level is precisely where the real power of mentorship is unlocked. Instead of breeding a codependent relationship in which the mentee simply continues to need you, outstanding mentors teach their mentees the skills necessary to do it themselves.

While I am still on a path to incorporating this into my life, I'd like to offer an interesting model that Joe has incorporated into his. He uses his sphere of influence as the chairman of a large manufacturing holding company to mentor at what Maimonides would consider the highest level. He identifies and hires diverse talent to manage his companies. He persistently invests in this talent, setting up opportunities for those who rise to the top to gradually buy him out of a major stake in the company. He gives the newly emerged wave of talent the keys to the purse, and the power to make decisions. He gives them equity in the business and skin in the game. Because he can't shake his Army discipline and still goes to the office at six AM on most weekdays, he's around to "catch them if they fall."

I strive to have a platform that is big and lucrative enough to do the same. I can think of few things that are more sustainability-focused than training the next generation to build.

Takeaway: Equipping someone else with the skillset to do whatever they aspire to is the highest form of mentorship. Strive to be that kind of mentor.

Effective Community Organizing

Organizing the Black Community: For Us, By Us, in 2020 and Beyond

Now that we've gotten sustainable building across the personal and professional domains out of the way, let me stir the pot with my views and concerns on building sustainably at the community level. It's impossible to be black in June 2020 and not contemplate what the future holds for all of us. As the most unexpected white faces emerge to chant "Black Lives Matter" in protest, I wake up worried almost every day. I worry that when posting a symbolic black box on social media is no longer trendy, this moment in time won't actually result in the material changes that the black community—and our country—need to ensure that there is truly one America.

The concept of one America not only pays homage to Dr. Martin Luther King Jr.'s 1967 speech at Stanford University, but its core message is also the story of our community's life. There are two Americas—one that has access to opportunity, education, jobs, bank loans, and civil rights, and another that does not. Before any reader asks me or another black person this question, let me preemptively address it. The persistent nature of this reality is such that we can't just "move to a different neighborhood" or "dress or talk a certain way" or "stack a lot of degrees" out of it.

So, where do we go from here? How do we ride America's awakening to the point of tangible and useful reform? I believe the answer lies in effective grasstops organizing and leadership. I don't take anything away from grassroots organizing and want to give it well-deserved credit for so effectively moving the needle on equality in this country. In fact, in a world where information is highly democratized, I strongly believe that grassroots and grasstops organizers need to link hands in the name of progress.

All that said, I still view grasstops organizing as an area of higher return on investment for two main reasons.

First, grasstops organizers are typically diverse subject matter experts who already have the ear of decision-makers. They are capable of activating those relationships for causes that are important to them. Second, given that grasstops organizers are thought leaders in their respective domains, they also tend to be financially secure, enabling them to self-fund the organizing. But besides being professionally diverse and financially secure, the grasstops organizers of the black community in 2020 are going to have to be passionately and purposefully bipartisan.

For far too long, Democrats have taken the black vote for granted and postured as the only party that cares. Not only is this false, but it is also a setup for failure. Our community's well-being is way too important to leave to the devices of one party while this country continues to operate in a deeply two-party system.

Let's say that we manage to gather a bipartisan, strategically diverse group of grasstops organizers with expertise relevant to advancing the black community. How do we structure the effort and what do we focus on? I envision this as a network of grasstops lay leaders in lockstep partnership with a staff who is relatively lean. It is preferable that, as opposed to having one chief executive, the power at the helm is divided between two individuals.

I will even go so far as to suggest that it's more effective if the two individuals are a male and a female. There is a lot to be said about what female leadership adds to an executive team, but I'll summarize it by highlighting that the yin-yang nature of male and female interactions plays out in the professional realm, just as it does in the personal.

An Agenda
Beyond thinking about who is at the helm of the organization, its leadership needs to be agenda (or cause), not personality, driven. The black community has an extensive and familiar history with personality-based movements. No

one lives forever, and there is a ton of risk in building a movement as if they do. Some of our greatest leaders have been shot, have died naturally, or have fallen out of favor, and their movements lost steam accordingly. When a movement revolves around its cause relentlessly, there is a built-in succession mechanism because the mission is everyone's North Star.

All of this begs the question about such an organization's agenda. What agenda is compelling and effective enough to leave a black community that is significantly more self-reliant in a decade from now than it is today? I feel strongly that this agenda has to be legislative in nature. There are many ways to be pro-black, but I believe that legislative work has the highest return on investment. We can raise all the money for our community-based organizations—and we should—but on an effort-for-effort dollar basis, legislative impact that drives funds into our communities is significantly more impactful.

Our country's legislators can direct millions of dollars into our communities with the stroke of a pen. As I consider where to spend my money and time, I always land on organizations that drive legislative change. Our legislative agenda needs to be tight—no more than two or three asks at a time, focused on the same general topic. Important folks don't have the time or the attention span to process or act on more than three requests. Having an overarching topic that glues our requests together is of the essence because that topic will become our brand—it will become what we are known for. We need to aim for intense brand recognition, making ourselves every legislator's go-to on our overarching topic.

There is a chorus of black voices who have written on and spoken about what it would take to have the one America that Dr. King spoke about. I am convinced that it takes economic empowerment. In justifying this position, I am going to lean on the thoughts of a highly respected black pundit, Claud Anderson. His concept of PowerNomics is a package of principles and strategies that explain race and offer a guide for black Americans to become a more self-sufficient and economically competitive group in America.

In *PowerNomics,* Anderson contends that without a solid economic foundation, without communal wealth, black people can't have black communities; they can only have black neighborhoods. Anderson refers to group economics as the first, and foundational, story of a five-story house in a black community. We have to build our own businesses to get money, power, and respect. Once that is in place, we can add the bricks for a second story, and that is political influence. He claims that most folks have it wrong—they want to do politics before they do economics.

Anderson is vehement about advocating for strengthened economics before anything else. The idea is to use money and power from the economic foundation to influence election outcomes and, therefore, elected politicians to pass laws that benefit the black community. The third story of the house is about getting a handle on our community's police force. We use politicians and our economic power to control how cops act in our streets, how judges treat black people in the courts, and to ensure a sense of fairness in the sentencing process.

The fourth story focuses on owning our print and electronic media so as to control our narrative, promote our businesses, and galvanize effectively around our issues. The US has roughly twelve thousand radio stations; black folks own close to 1 percent of them. If we can't communicate, then we can't motivate. If we can't motivate, then we can't organize. The fifth story of the house is one of education. The key, Anderson argues, is to move away from the standardization of education and to focus on the specific needs and talents of black children instead. This will set off a cycle of nurturing black talent that is positioned to give back to the black community. In all his appearances, Anderson makes clear that none of this is possible without the economic foundation. Black money should "bounce," exchange hands, eight to ten times before leaving the black community. Hispanic money bounces six to seven times. Asian money bounces thirteen to fourteen times. Black money often doesn't bounce once—we make it and then channel it toward a white-owned establishment the first time we transact. This needs to change quickly, and the opportunities to do that are all around us. Both the editor and publisher of this book are intentionally black, for example, and I look forward to sharing its success with them.

So what are some examples of meaningful legislative items that can truly build economic empowerment in the black community? Two critical examples come to mind—home ownership and black-business ownership. What if we tasked the country with creating one million new black home-owners? We can do this by providing down-payment assist-ance, getting tons of unbanked black people banked and recognized by credit scoring companies, and by actually enforcing fair lending laws that have been defied for cen-turies.

What if we spurred the creation of more than one hundred thousand new black-owned small businesses? We can do this by establishing entrepreneur hubs across the country, increasing access to capital, supporting black-owned banks, and expanding procurement from black-owned businesses. I don't claim to present an exhaustive list, but I stand by the idea that it's hard for poor people to help poor people. Let's focus the new age of black community organizing on turning that predicament around.

Coalition Building

Few sustainable movements have been built without the contributions of other communities. In the civil rights movement, we linked hands with the Jewish community and laid the foundation for a historic friendship that still endures today. I want to emphasize that there is no shame in coalition building with others. If you don't want to view it as a moral imperative, then view it as a tactical strategy. If we are going to influence our legislators and decision-makers, we need to do so through activists who look and feel like them. While the number of legislators of color is growing, it is still small relative to other groups, including Jews. We can't do this effectively without getting other groups involved.

Coalition building isn't just about us and other communities. It is also about us from within. If we don't manage the generational clash of leadership staring us in the face in our own community, then we are shooting ourselves in the foot and acting in intellectual dishonesty. The rise of inspirational black leaders, like Congressman Hakeem Jeffries, has underscored this challenge. After watching one of Jeffries's media appearances, viewers will realize that he is rooted in principled pragmatism, authenticity, and facts. That cannot be said of all the black leaders who have fought for our rights in at least the second half of the twentieth century. This is not a knock on their accomplishments or convictions, but the world is changing, and we need to keep up.

Coalition building is a contact sport, not for the faint-hearted. On many days, it feels like pushing a boulder uphill. It needs to be approached with a keen sensitivity toward lived human experiences, from which it is impossible to separate for any party involved. What comes to mind immediately are the several unfinished conversations about the Honorable Minister Louis Farrakhan that I've had with a close Jewish friend.

The moment that the religious leader's name surfaces in our dialogue, I can see my friend get visibly uncomfortable. When this first happened, I didn't necessarily understand what was going on. The more I learned, the more I realized that my friend's father survived the Holocaust. Growing up, his dinner table conversations were about the horrors of that time period, so any mention of antisemitism is incredibly triggering. The feelings of discomfort preclude my friend from hearing that there are plenty of black folks with lived experiences of benefitting from the Nation of Islam. As difficult as it is, coalition building is about working toward a common goal while validating and respecting everyone's lived experiences.

It's been easy for me to contextualize my Jewish friend's pushback about the Nation of Islam not only because we have built so much personal goodwill but also because I've gained a deeper understanding of the wider Jewish community through an extensive number of interactions with its members. When the Flint water crisis erupted, my Jewish friend was one of the first to call. When he said he was there for me, he meant it, and his actions following accordingly. When I lost my phone in Israel, my Jewish friend and Israeli local literally activated his entire network, traversing the country to find it. I don't deny that activating a network in a country the size of New Jersey is obviously easier than doing so in New York City, but watching him move felt like humanity was at work.

If we are going to seize the moment and ensure that the true needs of the black community are met, we are going to have to act strategically, be organized, and work with others. Black contributions to America's culture in the past four hundred years have shaped it beyond measure. Let us make sure that we are prosperous enough to be that impactful in the four centuries to follow.

Chapter 6
Better by Mistake

"A loss ain't a loss, it's a lesson,
Appreciate the pain, it's a blessin'"
—Jay-Z, *Smile*

It was the kind of prematurely warm April day that all Michigan residents get overly happy about. We go from snow boots and parkas to T-shirts and flip-flops practically overnight. And if you've ever lived there, you know exactly what I am talking about.

I jogged behind my oldest daughter as she turned her kid bike wheels, finding balance on her own for the first time. I could feel her light up from the exhilaration of riding free, from the triumph of no longer needing her training wheels. I let her enjoy the moment, as my own mind rolled back to all of our conversations about her fear of falling, of failing. Time and time again, she would tell me that she was scared to pump her brakes too late or not to shift her body weight enough to make the turn smoothly. "Honor these mistakes," I'd tell her. "They will teach you how to ride that bike." When we were putting our bikes back in the garage that night, her eyes locked on mine, the smile on her face stretching ear to ear. She gave me an "I did it" head nod and walked into the house. At the time, Bella was only seven, but I felt as though she was able to see the value of making mistakes clearly in that moment. She realized that all of the falling and all the scraped knees paved the way for her newly acquired skill.

Like Bella, I've never liked falling. Some of my mistakes have been especially difficult to rebound from, as I ruminated on what I could have done differently for months, rehashing the blunder. I still can't say that I *never* get stuck on mistakes, but I've gotten much better at understanding the opportunities and silver linings in them. When I internalized that even the worst of losses hold lessons, I was able to reposition my mind to spend the time absorbing the lessons instead of crying over spilled milk. What follows is a mix of storytelling about my own shortcomings and some actionable takeaways for the reader, sprinkled with what you'll hopefully find to be words of motivation.

Let me open by saying that making mistakes quickly puts you in circles with the best. The trendsetters who have defined our culture and whose very shoulders we stand on as entrepreneurs, innovators, and game changers have seen the worst of it. Take Oprah. She wasn't always the media mogul sitting on *Fortune* magazine's List of Powerful Women that we know today, and definitely not during her years in Baltimore. On April 1, 1977, the general manager of Baltimore's WJZ station informed her that they were cutting her as co-anchor of the weekday newscast and demoting her to morning cut-ins. This was no April Fools' joke. She proceeded to cycle through a series of jobs from news writing to street reporting, none of which jived with her style because the reporting was surface-level, but she enjoyed involving herself in other people's stories. Her perceived missteps eventually led her to gold, as she was asked to cohost a morning talk show called *People Are Talking*. She found her element and the rest is history.

Similarly, Steve Jobs was fired from Apple, the very company he co-founded, in his thirties. At the time, it was a devastating blow that undoubtedly felt like it robbed him of his sole purpose in life. But even he claimed that it was the most productive and important time in his life. In a 2005 commencement address, he told the graduating seniors of Stanford University, "I didn't see it then, but it turned out that getting fired from Apple was the best thing that could have ever happened to me. The heaviness of being successful was replaced by the lightness of being a beginner again, less sure about everything. It freed me to enter into one of the most creative periods of my life."

These two stories don't even begin to count the mistakes that both have inevitably made *after* they grew into success—the bigger your stage, the bigger your mistakes.

It is against this backdrop that I want to tell you about my own mistakes, a few on my way to success and a few "should've-known-better" moments even after I had built several successful businesses. Some of these may feel like the answers were staring me right in the face as you read about them, but that's the interesting thing about mistakes: in the midst of making them, you have to find your own footing and see it for yourself. The universe of potential mistakes is quite infinite, so the point isn't to avoid every single one or even the ones that I've made, but rather to develop an appreciation for rebounding, learning the lessons, and applying them the next time.

Death by (Box) Cuts

My most egregious financial loss came on the back end of an investment in a box cutter business. The loss burned so badly because it was a drastic departure from the image I had of myself as someone who is savvy with money and good at financial decision-making. The idea was brought to me by my college barber, a good friend and a fellow Rattler, a term often used to describe FAMU students and alumni. His eyes lit up as he told me about just having locked up a patent on his new, cutting-edge box cutter design. He was familiar with my ability to turn ideas into profits and asked for my assistance with the business plan. After we worked on several drafts of the document, he came knocking for an investment. Without an ounce of hesitation, I poured $50,000 into the venture—the business plan had my touch all over it, and I was invested, literally and figuratively, in my friend's passion project.

As we took the idea to market, the realities of selling it were not what we envisioned. This was a fairly low-dollar, low-margin product, so we knew that we had to rack up volume to make money. The industry was saturated with long-standing vendor relationships that were proving nearly impossible to penetrate for a newcomer, especially when it came to big-box retailers like Home Depot, Walmart, and Target. The business was bleeding money, and what did I do? Double down on my investment. All we needed was a bit more capital to float us to our first big sale, I thought. Months later, the situation still hadn't course corrected. An investor approached my friend, waving a $1 million acquisition price for the entire venture. I tried to convince my friend to sell the sinking ship, but he refused. He was overly attached to the idea, without rhyme or reason. Street code says that you ride or die with your friends, so I put more chips on the table once again. They say "Go big or go home," and we definitely didn't go home when we should have.

Over time, I arrived at the decision to exit, but doing so was no easy feat for a variety of reasons. One of them was the way that my contract was legally structured. It granted a tricky right of first refusal (ROFR) to my partner, the primary owner of the business, to buy out anyone who wanted to exit, and it attached an annoyingly lengthy period of time for that right to be exercised. I waited it out, hands tied, doing everything I could to keep our friendship intact. When the ROFR window closed, and my partner still hadn't bought me out, I was stuck with the responsibility of finding someone else to purchase my stake. I finally sold my share for cents on the dollar, marking the start of the mental process to evaluate my own mistakes.

I first examined how I had made the investment—high on emotion and low on due diligence. I was far too over-indexed on my friend's dream, especially after helping him craft the business plan. Emotions are subjective, and while business can never be fully objective, market studies help trend in that direction. Had I done one, I would've quickly discovered how difficult it was for a new entrant to sell high volumes in the box cutter space.

Takeaway: Roll up your sleeves and do your due diligence. Being a supportive friend is great, but don't let emotions get the best of you.

In the backward-looking analysis, I spent a lot of time understanding why I doubled down when the business was failing instead of taking chips off the table. A large part of the answer lies in a well-known decision-making heuristic known as escalation of commitment. The field of behavioral economics is dedicated to how people make decisions. It has long been known that human decision-making is rife with shortcuts that help us act quicker, not better, even when we are aware of what the biases are. Understanding these biases can, however, move the needle on the margin.

The escalation of commitment bias is a behavior pattern in which an individual facing increasingly negative outcomes from a decision or an investment continues the behavior instead of altering course. When I read about this and other behavioral heuristics months after I sold my investment, I immediately wished that I had been armed with this information as I made my way through the situation. Sometimes just hearing an idea articulated in a different way can provide clarity.

Takeaway: Learn about behavioral biases. My behavior in the box cutter story is an example of one, but there are many others. The recency, anchoring, and confirmation biases are among the best known.

Since so much time has elapsed since the investment, I am now unafraid to confess that my escalation of commitment was driven by a deeply ingrained fear of making mistakes that was in my psyche then and that remains, to a lesser extent, in my psyche now. I was scared to be wrong about that investment. This doesn't happen by coincidence. Our society doesn't celebrate mistakes in any way—quite the opposite. Good students don't make mistakes on exams. Good children follow the rules. Good workers get it right the first time. All of this sounds great, but is a very inside-the-lines framework, plagued by hypocrisy. In those same schools and organizations where we are marked down for making mistakes, we also learn that people stumble on great inventions and ideas when given the space to make mistakes. Even Gandhi valued trial and error; he believed that "freedom isn't worth having if it doesn't include the freedom to make mistakes."

Why, then, don't we allow, much less encourage, making mistakes? Particularly in business, we shy away from them, and we fear that people will see a *faux pas* as incompetence. We get stuck in a mindset in which success is driven by our image as experts rather than as learners. Layer that with highly quantifiable measures of performance such as sales, profits, and shareholder returns, and it feels like there is no way out of this constraining psyche.

While I am not suggesting that performance metrics don't matter, I want to offer a more expansive view of business success that makes room for mistakes. Consider an alternative. What if, as business owners, we were to ask our employees what mistakes they committed because they dared to do something different? What did they learn as a result? What if we could institutionalize the art of making mistakes, introduce a process for the madness, and innovate the innovation process?

Have the nerve to encourage yourself and those around you to make mistakes.

Takeaway: Attempt to shed the stigma of making mistakes and incorporate the process of making them into your everyday life. Document every time that you're attempting to solve a problem, big or small. In the process, hold yourself accountable for making at least five mistakes. Write the five mistakes down. Trust me, if you aren't making mistakes, you aren't learning—or at least, you aren't learning enough.

In all honesty, it wasn't fun to lose hard-earned money in the six digits. There were days during which I wasn't sure that six digits was going to be rock bottom or if I was going to recover the investment at all. The hardest part wasn't even losing the money but rather the mental contortion around the "How did I get here?" thinking. So why do I discuss the benefits of making this mistake so adamantly? Because making it enabled me to confront my fear of failure. Losing that money became the foundation on which I built the resolve never to be in that position again.

You may never lose money on the scale that I did, but making some mistakes is inevitable. It is impossible to live otherwise, unless you live so cautiously that you might as well not have lived, in which case you've failed by default. I found myself on the other side of the box cutter story with an inner security to rebound from mistakes and with lessons that success couldn't have given me. Making mistakes taught me things about myself and about business that I couldn't necessarily internalize another way. And it showed me who was by my side to help, or at least offer to, when things got rough. The knowledge that I emerged wiser and stronger from a setback, big or small, means that I am more secure in my ability to persevere through adversity. This is a gift. Things painfully won are typically worth more than our degrees, our accolades, and the money in our bank account.

Takeaway: Life is difficult and complicated and beyond anyone's control. Rebounding from mistakes builds confidence and humility that enables you to survive its vicissitudes.

On a more practical note, I wrap up this story by highlighting the importance of having good legal advice. A quality lawyer won't replace your due diligence, but he or she will raise red flags in the governing contract. Had my contract for the investment not had a sticky right of first refusal (ROFR) clause, I could have gotten out earlier, preventing some, though not all, of the losses. Folks making their first couple of investments always want to skimp on legal fees—I relate to this more than ever. I'm pretty sure that I didn't have a lawyer look at that contract at all. In retrospect, I should have fought the urge and hired someone, ensuring that I was not just making the cheapest choice. With legal help (and many other facets of business), one gets what one pays for.

Facetiously, I advise my mentees to have a lawyer for their lawyers, a system of checks and balances to ensure that the best, most proper advice wins. Those starting out and bootstrapping don't need two layers of lawyers, but know that lawyers help and they are worth the money.

Takeaway: Legal help is important. Don't be cheap.

A Tale of Two Homes

In the spirit of vulnerability, this is another story that feels so crystal clear in its lessons today but that I failed to see entirely when I was going through it. I had just moved to Detroit, Michigan, to work for then-Mayor Kwame Kilpatrick. Detroit is about an hour's drive from my hometown of Flint, so for all intents and purposes, Detroit was a new city that I had to learn from scratch. In fact, I was neither familiar with living in Detroit nor with doing so on a government salary. Luckily, my real estate investments in college and my sheer lack of time to spend money while I was working for and traveling with Tavis Smiley allowed me to save an outsized amount for someone my age.

As the new boy on the block, I was so thrilled to see Detroit's low real estate prices that I decided to buy not one—but two—homes with cash, one home to live in and one home to party in. I wish that this were some joke out of a sitcom about excess, but this was real life. And because I didn't have monthly mortgage payments, I lived as though I had a ton of cash to spend on other things—eating out, partying, and exploring Detroit. I fell into a lifestyle that revolved around these three things but on a salary that couldn't keep up, especially after taxes. So I compensated. I drastically under-contributed to my 403(b) plan, the government's version of a retirement savings account, on a monthly basis, and I habitually drew on my savings to cover my credit card bills, leading to a cycle of mistakes.

I had a great credit score, so with reasonable mortgage rates, there was no reason not to finance at least one, if not both, of the homes that I purchased. This is a misstep that continues to hurt me now. Although I've always paid my bills on time, my credit won't move past high 700s because I hadn't made big purchases on credit earlier on. It took me too long to learn that good credit isn't just about good payment history—it is also about using it and managing to keep balances current and low. Second, who in G-d's name needs two homes at the ripe age of twenty-five? The answer is *no one*. There's a list of living situation suggestions that I would give someone of that age now: get a roommate; live with family; partner with someone and start a business instead. The world is an oyster when it comes to saving money at twenty-five.

With all that, I am proud to say that I was shrewd enough to keep my primary residence in confidence because I had another residence for hosting and partying (yes, that's sarcasm). What I didn't do was approach these purchases wisely. I didn't register that a major recession would send the value of downtown Detroit properties into freefall and that it was just around the corner. As the recession set in, both properties were appraised at less than half of what I had paid. It wasn't viable to keep holding onto them (there I go, working on my escalation of commitment), so I decided to cut my losses and sell, making back cents on the dollar, yet again.

Takeaway: Very rarely does a twenty-five-year-old need two homes, especially if one is for partying. Credit can and should work in your favor—not everything needs to be purchased in cash. I won't belabor the point of doing due diligence any further.

In addition to these poor acquisitions, I wasn't managing my daily cash flow well either. I didn't give my 403(b) plan nearly enough love, a pretty flagrant mistake, given that it was returning a consistent 8 percent the entire time I spent working in the mayor's office. I did this because I was convinced that I needed more money to feed my dining out and partying. The worst part was how late I realized this. I noticed the plan's return rate as I was rolling it over, months after starting to work for my next employer. Just think about how much more I could have saved, given the power of compound interest. My spending was exacerbated by the fact that I was tapping into my savings to enable it. There is no reason why anyone should touch savings for daily spending. If this is happening, something in the budget isn't working, and it's typically on the cash outflow side. Since then, I've reigned in my spending and leveled up my income, so much so that sometimes I can't believe how much useless money went out the door when I was younger.

Takeaway: Don't use savings to sustain your daily spending. If this is happening, reevaluate what you're spending on, and why.

Beyond bank account math, I realized that my larger perspective on what I chose to do with my time was misaligned. My consumption was at an all-time high; you name it—clothes, food, people (I'm being honest). Instead of developing myself, reading, acquiring new skills, reflecting, and decompressing, I was finding more and newer ways of bringing stress into my life. I wasn't sleeping nearly enough, waking up to hangovers more times than I could count. I wasn't donating nearly enough money to charity, lacking the self-fulfillment around giving that my parents had instilled in me growing up. If I had to compare that version of Jonathan to the newly minted FAMU graduate just three to four years prior, I would honestly say that I had regressed.

Detroit's renaissance hadn't yet begun, so the influx of talent that the city touts today didn't exist during the time I am describing. Suffice it to say, I was not the average one of my five closest friends—I was a big fish in a small pond, and it wasn't serving me well. While I could have been compensating for these circumstances, I was doing the bare minimum. It was a privilege to serve the people of Detroit through my role at the mayor's office, but my learning curve in that role plateaued long before I realized it and had the skills to do something about it. Simply put, I was wasting the most important thing I had, and that was time. Not just my money, but my time. To paraphrase the words of the late Chadwick Boseman, I was allowing the days to go by when I could have been putting them into becoming who I was supposed to become. This was a mistake that eclipsed most of my others, and I've since been on major guard about making it again.

Takeaway (perhaps the most important of all): Take advantage of the free time you have, especially before you take on major responsibilities, like children. Use that time for skills building and for emotional growth. Don't party or spend it away.

Strictly Business

The theme of doing business with a clear head, no matter your partner's actions, has come up in this book on several occasions, but this story really hammers it home. As a consultant, I've had numerous clients who decided to stop paying me because they had a change in circumstances, regardless of what our contract dictated. I've had others who have attempted to cut me out of deals that I've put together—that one has always felt like such an insult to my intelligence. In all these instances, I've led with a litigation-free resolution and have done my best to walk an honorable path, often putting relationships ahead of money. This is no coincidence, given how I was raised. For a prolonged period of time during his tenure at Greene Home for Funerals, my dad didn't take a paycheck, rerouting the money toward a fund for single parents who had lost children to street violence in Flint. Talk about doing the right thing and giving "your last" to those who are less fortunate.

But what happens when it's not your client, but rather a friend or a peer? What happens when someone is supposed to have your back in business but they don't?

As Detroit started to revitalize, the gaps in its social scene for young professionals were becoming apparent. We were looking for good vibes and classy opportunities to network. I've always been in the problem-solving lane, so I teamed up with a party promoter, who was also a friend, to create Detroit Connect, a happy hour that would take place the first Monday of every month. He had the promoter's where-withal, while I found and contracted with our vendors, trademarked the name, and did the work to ensure that the series lived up to its reputation of connecting blue- and white-collar Detroiters, since we were living side-by-side in our neighborhoods. The city desperately needed this diplomacy, and I was excited about bridging the old and new versions of Detroit. After we had sold out several Mondays in a row, I was debriefing with one of the vendors, who innocently asked me if I had gotten a check. "What check?" I asked. "The checks that I've been cutting in [your partner's] name," he answered. There and then it hit me. My partner was getting paid, without giving me my share.

It would have been simple to give into the urge to call him and go off or to drive to his house and handle it in person, like a man. Instead, I decided to sit on it. I accept that not everyone loves and follows mafia movies like I do, but when did Don Corleone ever lose his cool in *The Godfather?* I was determined to emulate his calm and collected demeanor and to strategize before I acted in anger. That evening, I slept on it. The morning brought me conviction, clarity, and resolve, as it typically does. I called my partner, expressed my disappointment, and asked to close shop on the operation. I didn't even ask for my share of the money, though he tried to offer it out of guilt, naming every excuse in the book about neglecting to pay me. I didn't need to take the money: I owned the trademark for the series' name—my now ex-partner knew he couldn't continue without that, and hence, without me.

Looking back, I should have been more discerning about who I partnered with, especially on a voluntary basis. You don't always choose your primary income-producing clients, but you have more latitude with community projects. The years have taught me to be less trusting. Although my word and my handshake are as bullet-proof as a fair contract, I've learned that this is not the standard used by many others. I am proud that I handled the Detroit Connect situation honorably, acting with good intent. The world conspires in your favor when your intentions are pure, allowing you to both enter and exit situations.

Lastly, and quite obviously, protect your intellectual property! The simplest names, logos, and taglines can end up being highly coveted assets over night. It may not feel convenient to fork up the trademark filing fees when something is just getting started, but it can save a lot of heartache down the road. It deserves to be highlighted that I felt more comfortable exiting this partnership than my box cutter investment because our legal contract was crafted with professionalism. I put my own lesson into practice and paid a lawyer to review it. The circumstances I described fit right into one of the contract's allowable termination conditions. So besides our gentlemanly conversation, I wrote my partner a notice of termination that dissolved the contract in seven days. If nothing else, it felt good to know that I was learning.

Besides which, this was strictly business, and that should never unsettle a person grounded in morality.

Takeaway: Think before you act, so that you don't act from a place of anger or emotion. When you do act, don't abandon your principles of honor, and don't stop treating folks how you want to be treated. Someone else's behavior should never be your moral barometer.

Given a Time Turner, I would tell the Jonathan that landed in Detroit at twenty-four that life is not a checklist of acquisitions or achievements. Your qualifications, your resume, are not your life, I would say, though there are many folks who confuse the two. How you rebound from mistakes, how you put learned lessons to work, how you treat people when you're not pleased with their behavior—*that* is your life; *that* is your character.

I am infinitely thankful for my mistakes. While these stories aren't even the tip of the iceberg when it comes to the sheer number (we'd need a separate book for that), they do highlight the character building that mistakes have ushered into my life. They have been an integral part of my path, and recognizing them as such has given me the mental strength and freedom to get to the very intersection of business and social impact that this book is about.

I'm better by mistake.

Chapter 7
Making Dollars While Making Change

It's a choice and you make it every day.
—Jonathan Quarles

I vividly remember the meeting with one of my challenging clients that changed my life. The management team was tough as nails to navigate, but I look back on what we accomplished together with pride. The BTL Group is my longest-standing entrepreneurial venture. It has had an interesting and fulfilling journey, which I'll discuss later in this chapter, but for the purpose of this story, you simply need to know that The BTL Group is a business development and relationship management platform.

Several years ago, per former Michigan Governor Rick Snyder's recommendation, I was approached by a large Indian information technology (IT) company whose US office was based in Michigan. It was making $100 million in top-line revenue and had mastered the delivery of a wide array of IT services. The company was looking to expand its pool of government contracts, especially in its home state.

After reflecting on the company's goals for a few days, I presented the leaders with a comprehensive strategic plan that entailed a meaningful philanthropic component. By this point, The BTL Group was a well-established, reputable operation, so I had no qualms with charging a steep, but fair, price for my services. From the first meeting, I could tell that the management team was processing the information that I put in front of them with a mix of surprise and confusion. My monthly retainer probably felt like a lot to swallow, and the company had no prior experiences with corporate philanthropy. The management team proceeded to do what most people do—play a game of hot potato. Instead of passing a hot potato, they were passing off the decision to hire me, and the hot potato theme song never seemed to stop.

After weeks of rotating meetings, I decided to confront the issue head-on. I had reached my walkaway point in our proverbial negotiation and asked for one final meeting with the CEO. I could feel the gravity of our cultural differences as I, a black man, looked an Indian man in the face and told him that he had to trust me. In a calm tone of conviction, I explained that if his company was going to double its business, it would have to approach clients in communities it had never worked in.

That was only going to happen with the use of pointed and methodical philanthropy. The company leaders needed to do something they had never done—invest wise charitable dollars—if they were going to get something they didn't have, a doubled top line. The only concession I offered for the sake of the management team's comfort, outside of all the face time that I'd already given the relationship, was a shorter-than-usual, three-month contract. "Let me de-risk the situation for you," I told the CEO. If I didn't hit my benchmarks after three months, he would be contractually allowed to cancel the contract. One day later, we signed.

By the time I exited the engagement a year later, not only was the client making $250 million in top-line revenue, but we deployed close to $200 thousand in targeted philanthropic dollars. The majority of these funds went to support the work of multiple community-based organizations in Wayne County, as my client relentlessly pursued and landed a sizable opportunity with Wayne County IT services. I was pleased with the former, but I was incredibly proud of the latter. The client accomplished its financial goals at a relatively low price while I got to unlock $200 thousand of new charitable giving and own all the relationships in the process.

I carry this story as my own reminder of the difficulties associated with intersecting business and social impact. It's hard but rewarding. More important, it's a choice I make every single day. Entrepreneurs who live at this intersection may feel like they're doing it against all odds, but it does get easier when we incorporate several important ideas into the process.

The New Entrepreneur Thinks Globally

It starts with a global mindset. I talked a bit about coming into my own about the global nature of our world in Chapter 3 when I studied abroad in South Africa. Since then, I've truly done my best not just to enjoy travel, but to live it as a value. What do I mean by living travel as a value? I mean traveling to actively learn. I've never looked at travel as a way to replicate my American sense of comfort or my American reality. Instead, I've opened myself to the natural discomfort that comes with immersive experiences away from home. It almost always leads me to a better version of myself.

Global exploration has also taught me to seek truth beyond the media coverage or the historical fiction novels. In my experience, the reality of most traveled places doesn't look like the TV footage. Instead, it is more raw—more authentic. Every time that I've forged relationships while traveling, I've felt authentic reciprocity. Now, when I interact with challenging clients from different cultures, I lean on one of my most important lessons from traveling—we are all connected by a basic human need to be heard and affirmed. If and when in doubt about this, you can always pop open the one acceptable book on travel abroad to alleviate your anxiety— *Kiss, Bow, or Shake Hands: The Bestselling Guide to Doing Business in More than Sixty Countries* by Terri Morrison and Wayne A. Conaway.

The more that you adopt travel as a value, the better you become at being uncomfortable. I have no doubt that there was a direct correlation between my extensive body of travel experiences and my ability to level with the Indian CEO of that IT company. You will never know everything about a culture, but you become increasingly more socially agile—

the non-verbal cues begin to make more sense, and you decipher the messages in them more quickly. You also come to manage your own discomfort about cultural differences more efficiently, enabling you to lead folks to your desired outcomes more deftly. I am not sure that the Jonathan of fifteen years ago could've held his ground in that meeting as firmly and as confidently as the one on the other side of all the travel adventures.

The pragmatic aspect of cultural economics has never been lost on me and shouldn't be lost on you either. The entrepreneur of tomorrow will have to work in and with other countries or he/she will be left behind. If you want to do business in Asia's relationship-based commercial ecosystem, you can't start the day you decide. Your Asian clients and counterparts will need to trust you. Trust takes time, and it takes a social agility muscle that gets reps when you live travel as a value.

The world is catching on quickly. Give it another five years and heightened global awareness will no longer be a competitive edge. Rather, it's going to be the great equalizer. The onus is on us not only to expose our kids to the world, but to also gift them the tools to interact with it. If we are going to breed the next generation of game changers, let's advocate for the rollout of mandatory immersive language and study abroad programs as early as elementary school.

While we are doing that, let's not forget the abundance of creative ways to travel for free so that money is never the bottleneck.

As I continue to live travel as a value, I've learned that reciprocity on my own turf is just as crucial. In that spirit, I am equally as passionate about being a generous domestic host as I am about traveling abroad. Interestingly, being a good host, especially for large foreign delegations, is a lot more about the preparation process than it is about the actual gathering.

The best resource I've found for doing this effectively, outside of practice, is a book written by Priya Parker, a fellow Coca-Cola Scholar and friend, *The Art of Gathering: How We Meet and Why It Matters*. Priya advocates for hosting with a script. She emphasizes the importance of the due diligence leading up to the gathering. She stresses the details—the seating arrangements matter, the ice breakers need to be thoughtful, as does the approach to culture sharing. I admit that before encountering Priya's work, I was a lot less calculated in my approach to hosting, especially given how much I did it. Now, I widely recommend Priya's book. Give it a whirl. I promise you won't regret it.

Problem-Solve with a Purpose

Seeking to problem-solve with a purpose must be at your core. Entrepreneurs have to be problem-solvers at heart, but

I've always viewed problem-solving as a means to an end. As the sun was setting on time in corporate America, I contemplated a straightforward path, which would have been to start a one-man lobbying firm. Quickly, I realized that I didn't have to do what everyone else was doing. Instead, I wanted to tap into a market problem, the solution to which was going to place me at the intersection of my passion and my purpose, which wasn't necessarily pure lobbying.

Early on, I understood that whatever I was going to do wasn't meant to be just about changing business or a market. It was going to be about changing the narrative and being a part of something larger than myself. I also knew that it was going to revolve around people. Many years since Tavis Smiley dubbed me "JQ Smooth," I've embraced the spirit of that nickname. I've always had a knack for connecting with, and relating to, folks from different walks of life. To me, there was simply no business without people. The BTL Group ended up being a convergence of all these things, and a project of real self-actualization. Even on my toughest days, I feel fulfilled in a way that I've always dreamed about, with a lifestyle that's as flexible as the one that I've always wanted.

Common Link Consulting Services was The BTL Group's forerunner. I was a college sophomore when I formed

Common Link as an avenue for my passion projects. FAMU, my alma mater, was Common Link's first meaningful client. After completing a summer as a Coca-Cola scholar intern in Atlanta, I returned to campus only to find that many dorms had no vending machines. Addressing this market void, I leveraged my relationships from the summer to help the university cut a deal that made sense. Subsequently, FAMU hired me as its student lobbyist. My intentionality about making dollars while making change was not nearly as well articulated back then, but doing that work on behalf of the school was probably my first go at tying business to social good.

Common Link's second significant client was Tavis Smiley's Foundation. As I mentioned in Chapter 2, my work as his youth ambassador persisted all throughout college. Also during my internship at Coca-Cola Scholars Foundation, I peeped that the company was being widely scrutinized for its shortcomings about the promotion of underrepresented minorities. Simultaneously, Tavis's foundation was looking for corporate sponsors, and it occurred to me that the pairing could be a real win for both parties.

Coca-Cola Foundation was going to be able to tell its investors a story about backing one of the most credible black voices of the time, while Tavis's foundation was going to get additional resources to continue its outreach to thousands of young men and women of color. With the help of my mentor at Coca-Cola Foundation, Ingrid, I was able to connect the two parties, and the sponsorship happened exactly as I envisioned. I rebranded Common Link Consulting Services into The BTL Group in 2014, but the work I did through it helped me develop both conviction in and early proof of concept for making dollars while making change.

The decade after college was filled with jobs that all had me reporting to a boss or to several. I reflect on those years as a period of skill building—a down payment of sorts on the rest of my life. The BTL Group quietly existed in the background, sometimes as nothing more than a subliminal reminder that using business as a conduit for social impact was possible and sometimes to help local nonprofit organizations in my area.

In the year 2014, I decided to strike out on my own, making The BTL Group my vehicle. I had already been doing the work that became The BTL Group's bread and butter for other people, so I rolled the dice. Among other things, I was motivated by the ability to connect with a self-directed purpose and the prospect of being a more present father.

Amidst all the debate about whether or not women can "have it all," fatherhood has often felt like an extinct conversation, but the tides have slowly been turning. Not only is the importance of dads emerging from negligence as a field of study, but it's always been personal for me. In a world that largely socializes men to be providers, while leaving the duties of childcare to women, I've pushed myself to be a loving, present father since the day each of my girls was born. To be fair, I've had zero excuses to be anything but given my father's blueprint for parenting. Besides having my own father as an example, I've tried to elevate the standard even further. The Black Panthers' most meaningful legacy may be tied to civil rights, but I've spent a lot of time considering their ideology on parenting—"A man that has not prepared his children for his own death has failed as a father." I view my kids' mental, spiritual, and financial independence and well-being as my ultimate test, and I drive toward that every day that I'm with them. I don't claim to do it perfectly, but I'll take credit for the intentionality. When asked if men can have it all, my answer is still that "yes, they can." Doing it all lies in reimagining success. Leaning into The BTL Group was one way of doing that.

The BTL Group

In my purpose-driven vision of The BTL Group, I wanted to fuse my ability to build bridges between people and ideas with my business acumen. In my business-driven vision of The BTL Group, I wanted to address a thorny market inefficiency among sales organizations at the time. The economy was just reemerging from the turmoil of the 2007–

2008 financial crash. Companies were being cautious about growth and conservative about costs. They were unwilling to bloat their sales departments to pre-2008 levels, especially because each hired sales rep meant an upfront investment in training and a long ramp-up period.

The core value proposition of The BTL Group was as an outsourced sales department with minimal risk to any given client. I wasn't asking for health insurance or for office space. I charged a monthly retainer per a contract that could be canceled at any point, and there were plenty of points—I was being evaluated rigorously every month. While each client I took on worked in a different area, my learning curve was still quicker than that of most salaried reps because I sold diverse products and ideas in my former roles.

I enjoyed this work on a personal level as it kept me sharp and engaged in a variety of industries, as opposed to feeling the stagnation that inevitably creeps up with focusing on just one. I hope you can appreciate the reference to the TV drama *Scandal*, when I say that I spent The BTL Group's early years building its brand as the "Olivia Pope" of sales. But even as I did this, I never lost sight of the ultimate goal, which was to position it as a platform that made as much change as it did dollars.

The year of 2016 was another monumental year in The BTL Group's trajectory. President Donald Trump was elected and his inward-facing, US-centric approach to immigration was evident immediately. I quickly connected the dots on what this could mean for international companies exploring business opportunities in the US—their lives were about to get significantly harder. Luckily, I had been traveling abroad and forging relationships for years, so I was well positioned to capitalize on what was about to happen.

Slowly but surely, this movie played out just as I predicted. One by one, clients outside the US began approaching me about helping them break into US markets. I started to lightly dabble in the work, remaining vigilant of the differences in the way commerce was conducted across countries. A year in, I realized that international clients often made for better clients. They paid their bills, and, in my experience, they rarely had a chip on their shoulders about doing my job better than I could.

The COVID-19 pandemic threw an even bigger wrench in the ability of my international clients to tend to their US affairs. This further drove the value of having a US-based advisor, highlighting the indispensable nature of The BTL Group. In the four years since I was hired by my first international client, The BTL Group's geographic footprint outside the US has expanded in ways that I could have never anticipated. This geographic diversification has also shielded the business from the kind of losses experienced by entrepreneurs with solely US clients. I am mostly thankful to my client base outside the US for making me a better international thinker and student, for helping me be more relevant in a world that's flat, and for opening my eyes to innovation that has far outpaced that in the US.

Quartz Water Source

Innovation outside the US is an important topic worthy of further discussion. There is a saying that "necessity is the mother of invention." What I've seen is that other countries often encounter their "necessities" before the US and conjure better, more developed solutions to what end up being our shared challenges. Having a mind that's as open to international innovation as it is to that of domestic has helped me bring more value to my clients, my community, and my country. The creation of Quartz Water Source grew out of my consulting work with The BTL Group, but it is really a story about problem-solving for the best solution, finding it abroad, and learning to evangelize it.

The notorious Flint water crisis first made headlines in 2014, though my involvement with water issues didn't begin until 2018. By then, I couldn't continue to sit on the sidelines as the crisis decimated the spirit, health, and economy of my hometown. Flint was growing its graveyard of one-off "Band-Aid" solutions to its problem with clean drinking water, but none seemed to answer the call in sustainability or scalability.

Organized trips to Israel tend to incorporate aspects of the country's longstanding history of water innovation and thought leadership. It was no surprise that on one such trip, I stumbled on a variety of cutting-edge water technologies in filtration, irrigation and water generation. It was inspiring to witness how a country located in such an arid environment had turned its weather and natural resource conditions into a force for groundbreaking advancements. As I wrapped my mind around all the moving pieces of the crisis facing Flint, I began to realize that the city could meaningfully benefit from a few of the solutions that I encountered in Israel.

Simultaneously, exponential spikes in coronavirus infection rates brought the country's economy to a screeching halt, state by state. As no one knew what the future would hold for existing businesses, I was definitely at a loss around what it would look like to launch a company on the other side of the country's stay-at-home order. So I drew inspiration and wisdom from where I always draw it—in helping my community, in my 'why'—using entrepreneurship for social good, and in a degree of blind faith that the universe would serve me the guidance I needed. Interestingly enough, while shutting down the economy, coronavirus also spotlighted the importance of access to clean water and motivated me to work harder. Short of a vaccine, hygiene became the most potent weapon against the virus. In communities plagued by contaminated water or water shutoffs, hygiene was a rare privilege, not a basic right. Combining these domestic challenges with the global nature of the water crisis, I felt the burning need to launch Quartz Water Source in August 2020.

Today, Quartz thinks of itself as a hub for 'second-line' clean water solutions, while it works to create a global market for alternatives to municipal water. No matter where the journey takes Quartz, I find comfort in knowing that its founding is the epitome of using business for good. The setbacks so far have paled in comparison to the potential of using innovative water technology to create more self-reliant communities and to put a real dent in the global water crisis.

There is no doubt that making dollars while making change becomes easier the more successful you are. When I first formalized The BTL Group, I had to work with whoever was willing to pay for my services just to keep the lights on. But success is a funny thing because it usually begets more success. The more client goals that I crossed off the list, the more clients came knocking, and the choosier I became. Today, The BTL Group doesn't sign clients who aren't willing to invest in some kind of philanthropic component. Financial success doesn't hurt either. As the water company's sole owner, I had to put up the seed capital. I say all this with the full understanding that while it's a blessing to be in this position, it's a duty to perpetuate it.

An Opportunity in Cannabis

A fierce sense of intentionality makes living at the intersection of business and social impact easier. Six months ago, I was approached by a cannabis lifestyle brand looking to use The BTL Group's services to "undo a knot" in the city of Detroit. The company found itself in an unfortunate set of relationship circumstances with the wrong people. I could tell that it desperately needed the help, displaying a willingness to pay almost any price.

I liked the business, but I had a different plan. I asked the chief financial officer (CFO) for a couple of days to gather my thoughts and to capitalize on his curiosity. I believed in the future of the cannabis industry and used the time to research Michigan's competitive landscape in the sector. My research confirmed that this company had a recognizable brand and a superior product. I was also intrigued by its contemplated commitment to hiring and training ex-convicts with minor recreational and medical marijuana sentences. Black and brown folks are severely overrepresented in this group.

I came back to the CFO with a three-pronged counterproposal. Prong one was my agreement to lend The BTL Group's services to the situation and to be compensated accordingly. Prong two was a request to be at the table. I wanted to become an equity owner of the cannabis company. In return, I promised to syndicate a large chunk of money for my equity stake from investors in the black community. The cannabis business was going to pay me a fundraising fee in the amount of a certain percentage of all money raised. Prong three was a request to be named an officer of the company in charge of overseeing its social equity programs and strategic community partnerships up and down the supply chain.

Recognizing that my request was bold, the CFO agreed to my counterproposal, contingent on my ability to raise the capital. Likely attempting to undermine, he proceeded to inform me that no African American he had approached was willing to invest in the company. He was partially right—no real precedent existed for black equity ownership of a sizable cannabis company in Michigan. But I also had a feeling he wasn't asking the right people.

Walking out of that meeting, I had a loosely defined strategy about potential investors, and I knew that putting my own skin in the game would make a real difference. However, I definitely didn't have all the capital and my ability to raise the difference didn't necessarily feel like a foregone conclusion. What I did have was a strong sense of conviction in the importance of black ownership and a deep sense of purpose around using a business I believed in as a conduit for positive impact in a community that I belonged to. I was unequivocal about making dollars while making change.

In just thirty days, I raised the capital and all three prongs of my proposal are in full swing today. I recently helped the company develop a relationship with an obstinate mayor who wasn't supportive of the cannabis industry. I articulated what interested me about the business and showed up for her in ways that she needed politically. When she was looking to distribute additional COVID-19 protective equipment to parts of her city, the cannabis company subsidized the equipment while I distributed it with her.

This story is not about highlighting the door-opening power of capital that we already know—a power missing in most pockets of the black community. Rather, this story under-scores the intentionality of using business for good, the impact of setting your mind to something, and the impor-tance of dictating your own game rules instead of accepting those given to you.

Twenty years ago, social impact felt like a thing left to the do-gooders, while profitable business was a domain for the capitalists. As new impact investing strategies and corporate social responsibility departments pop up every day, the narrative is changing, and it is doing so rapidly. A friend told me that there are five kinds of social entrepreneurs—a *founder*, who starts for-profit and nonprofit organizations seeking to change the world; a *disruptor*, who shakes up the status quo and drives systemic change; an *intrapreneur*, who leverages status and resources from within an establishment to drive social impact solutions; an *influencer*, who has the ability to amplify awareness and mobilize others to take action; and an *investor*, who uses financial and social capital to create change.

On my personal journey of entrepreneurship, I have been every one of the five. From experience, I can say that each one is greater than the sum of its parts, and each one has a part to play in bettering the world. Whichever kind of entrepreneur resonates with you, the work ahead is meaningful, yet abundant, and the barriers to doing it are lower than they have ever been.

To all my aspiring game changers—I hope this book nudged you out of your respective comfort zones and gave you real food for thought.

To all my game changers—I hope this book is your call to action. The wind is at your backs. There has never been a better time to make dollars while making change.

A Letter to My Younger Self

In the reflective spirit of this book, here are some thoughts that summarize the past and present, and which I lean on as inspiration for the future.

Dear Younger JQ.

You may have never seen yourself as a good enough writer, but you will publish a book (or several). It'll be hard work, but believe it or not, you'll find it incredibly therapeutic, and its completion will happen at the perfect time. As life goes on, you'll discover that you do your best work when you're purpose driven and motivated by the idea that your talents and blessings don't belong to you. They are on loan from the Creator, and it's your duty and privilege to share them with the world. The book will be one of your avenues for doing just that.

Since this is a letter to your younger self, I feel that it's most appropriate to tell you that (your) youth does not have to be wasted on the young. By the time you read this, you will have indulged in so much excess — partying, spending, shopping, consuming. No matter what you've convinced yourself of, that hangover is never worth it. Instead, go to bed early and wake up early. Your rest is important. You're probably doing your hardest not to be up at this hour, but the most productive time is between 5:00 and 6:30 AM. Being up before everyone else, even before the sun, puts

you in control of your day, a feeling that

you'll find liberating as you grow older.

Speaking of time, protect yours.

"No" is a complete sentence, and you

should speak it more often. You may feel

that saying "yes" to every direction you're

pulled in makes people like you, but boy

can I tell you how little that actually

matters. Since time is the one thing you can't get back, focus it on building your vision, developing yourself, and finding your own sense of fulfillment. I am not encouraging you to be selfish, but I am encouraging you to be selective. Folks will love to talk to you about balance. Let me reality check by saying that balance in a moment is an illusion. Sometimes work will get the short end of the stick and sometimes play will. The closest you can hope to get to balance is a 50 / 50 in the long run.

In case you haven't gotten the point yet, invest in yourself mentally, physically, spiritually, and financially. If you don't invest in yourself, how can you expect anyone else to? Shore up seed money for your ventures — it'll keep you committed. Learn the nooks and crannies of your business and its supply chain. Very few people will care about it the way you do. and you're less likely to get cheated out of money if you know what you're doing. You're a serial entrepreneur. and that's not going to change. In fact. you will have started twelve businesses by the time you're forty. The road is going to be windy and bumpy. Don't forget to celebrate the small wins. They matter just as much as, if not more than, the big ones. Have a life partner who cares about the small wins and who is genuinely proud of you every single day.

Sitting where you are, you probably

think that you can vacation and refuel when you die. How can you not? Your generation damn near pioneered the concept of "FOMO" — fear of missing out. So let me answer that with another shorthand: "F*ck That Sh%t." Your mind, your creative spirit, and your body need to recharge so that you can walk with purpose and with your best foot forward. You might have noticed this letter's emphasis on the word purpose—coincidentally. this is on purpose (yes. pun intended). Purpose gets you through the lows. through the days when nothing feels like it's going right. Your purpose is your why. a powerful notion that's linked to your values and that cuts through all the hows. You'll define and redefine your purpose several times, but it'll always be tied to using your gifts to better your community and the world. One marker of having your purpose is a sense of comfort with your authentic self. Hold onto that comfort, even at the risk of being misunderstood. Living to impress or appease others is a futile strategy, bound to crumble like a house of cards, given the first sighting of an obstacle.

As both your biggest critic and number-one fan. I feel obliged to highlight the incredible trail that you've already blazed by being your authentic self. Remember the time you spent in aerospace and defense lobbying? You would come down to the manufacturing floor. heads turning with confusion and surprise. as folks looked at you. the youngest and only Black executive at the firm. They did everything they could to undermine you—cut you out of opportunities. Talk behind your back—sending over and over the message that you're too young and it's too soon. You were steadfast and undeterred. You learned the industry quickly. you wore a smile on your face daily. and you killed them with kindness. You won your worst enemies over. turning their jealousy of your trajectory into mutual understanding. You walked with kings and queens, but you never lost the common touch.

You might love being the life of the party, but it is tiring as hell, and I need you to get out of the habit of focusing on what's hot right now. You will witness many peers, friends, and associates flare out just as quickly as they flared up. Be different. Seek to be forever. Slow and steady progress should be your aim, and if the progress feels too slow, as it sometimes will, trust the process. Patience is a virtue. There will be times when you won't fully understand what to make of someone's motivation, of a relationship, or of a connection. Be still and let time do its work to bring you the clarity that only time can. Deal making gets a carve-out. Go carefully but swiftly after the business you want to do, because time can kill deals.

By now, you've grown into Tavis Smiley's nickname for you, "JQ Smooth." Even fifteen years later, your ability to connect with people will remain one of your superpowers. Like all power. I caution you to wield it wisely. Do not be transactional and do not use it to manipulate. Both of those things harm you more than anyone else — they leave you feeling empty. Here's one sure way to avoid that. Use that superpower to do one thing daily that scares you or that creates magic in someone else's life instead.

Dad always taught you not to mistake your presence for power. "The mere fact that you're able to serve is the gift in of itself." he'd say, and you should cherish it infinitely. I am proud of you for the several important instances during which you've upheld this principle honorably. Your time with former Mayor Kwame Kilpatrick could have had you riding high; you had every city service, department, and government connection right at your fingertips. You could have easily disregarded the annoying complaints, the personal cries for help, from citizens who were looking to you to solve problems that you never had a hand in creating. Instead, you answered the calls, the pleas, and the letters, putting humanity ahead of everything else. Thank you, Younger JQ, for living up to your father's expectations. It is no wonder that you were never associated with the perceived flaws in Kilpatrick's administration, and may you never forget this lesson.

Learn to differentiate what's in your sphere of control and what isn't. Focus on only the things you can control.

Weaknesses go in the same bucket. You can't spend too much time worrying about them. There's a line between self-improvement and an unnecessary fixation on weakness. It will become clearer to you over time. Set yourself up to outsource the things you don't like to do, the things you consider low value, and the things that you are not good at. Pay the folks doing them their fair value. Don't be cheap, because you will get what you pay for.

If you're going to pay others their fair value, you should know your own. Once you've gotten clear on it, be sure to add a tax. In a world that always wants discounts, don't give anyone the wholesale version. Continue to increase your value relentlessly — learning from others is one fruitful way of doing that. Intentionally sit at the feet of elders and seasoned change makers. Come prepared to listen. You've already missed some great opportunities to do that, and I don't want you to miss many more.

Similarly, purge the folks whom you don't feel like you're learning from at all, or those who no longer serve your higher self. Your higher self is a complicated concept, to which you can (and just might) dedicate a different book, but you sometimes know it when you feel it. Start by taking stock of how you feel around certain people. Pay attention to whom you're with when you feel your best. In your gut, you know who needs to go; you're just afraid to pull the trigger.

Don't be. It's a healthy part of your evolution. And if you're not evolving, then you're stagnant — a place worse than failure.

While we're on the topic of purging things, debt would be a good thing to purge as well. Some debt is okay, but not at the expense of your financial health. The next recession is inevitably going to happen, and you'll want to be liquid when it does. You don't get access to other people's money if your credit score is subpar. You'll go on to make some really stupid financial decisions only to learn that you should exhaust the options of using other people's money before dipping into your own. The same goes for business. There's a sea of pitch competitions and small business grants.

especially when a recession wakes large companies up to the importance of social responsibility. Don't sleep on those opportunities. As you're out pursuing these, remember that the culture of your company matters more than just about anything else regarding the business. Culture eats strategy all day. You know what eats culture though? Sending inappropriate texts or emails — like the kind you'd never want your loved ones to see. Don't let the infinite nature of your electronic footprint become your Achilles' heel.

I've always told you not to make important decisions long after sunset or shortly after dawn. And that is still true. Yet the most reliable overall guide to choice is to follow whatever makes you feel happy and excited to get out of bed in the morning. Life is not supposed to be a grim slog of discipline and sacrifice. Leave that for the folks who aren't masters of their own fate, the way you are. Let your compass be an overwhelming sense of gratitude, joy, love, and whatever else makes you feel alive.

I'll leave you with one last parting

thought: some major things won't turn out the way you expected. You're going to wrestle with the discomfort. searching for answers. You're going to rehash your role in it. seeking to understand how it could have happened to you. Rest assured that you were meant to go through it so you can unlock the deepest gifts of your destiny and that you will emerge on the other side happier than you ever

imagined.

Your biggest supporter.

JQ

Appendix

While the entire book was intended to be prescriptive, the appendix is really meant to close the gap between theory and practice. In it, I share some of the tips, tricks, products, and processes that have helped me along my entrepreneurial journey. For ease of use, the information is broken down by chapter number and topic.

Chapter 4

I. **Peak Performance Diet:** Diet is trial and error, so I've done a lot of experimenting over the years. Below are some of my findings.

   a. There is a large body of research on **intermittent fasting,** the practice of eating only within a strict eight-hour window. I haven't always stuck to it perfectly but when I have, my energy levels have often been higher. I'll typically eat from noon to eight PM. When I do, I drink a ton of water in the morning to avoid feeling hungry.

   b. Meals consist of the following foods:
- **Lunch includes colorful vegetables** (spinach, carrots, broccoli, etc.).
- **Lunch includes a protein.**

- I prefer fish. For a while I didn't like the heaviness of beef in my stomach, but after exploring blood-type based dieting, I learned that, given my blood type, I need to consume more red meat.
- **Dinner is solely comprised of vegetables.**
  - No one's body enjoys breaking down complex proteins in the second half of the day, so I stay away from proteins in the evening.

c. Other foods for high performance are the following: **seaweed,** a rich source of brain-boosting omega-3 fatty acids; **avocado,** full of healthy fats and good for blood flow; **sea moss gel** and **bladderwrack,** both immune system-boosting agents.

II. **Supplements:** I am generally a believer in the idea that we should be able to get all of our nutrients from the food we eat. But given my fast-paced days and demanding schedule, I try to leave little to chance. Here are some products that you'll find in my medicine cabinet:

a. **Restore Complete Gut Well-Being:** Helps clean out the gut.

b. **Live Probiotics:** Promotes regularity in bowel movement.

c. **Coconut Oil Pulling:** Removes toxins from both the mouth and tongue, especially after a night of smoking or drinking.

d. **Other Helpful Supplements**
   - Wholemega Fish Oil
   - Vitamin C
   - Vitamin D3 + Vitamin K2
   - Men's Multivitamin
   - Aged Garlic Extract (great for heart health and lowering cholesterol)
   - Turmeric

e. **Potent Detox Treatments**
   - Celery, carrot, apple, and ginger juice
   - Apple cider vinegar, cinnamon, honey, lemon, cayenne pepper, and turmeric, all taken an hour before my meal to cleanse and speed up digestion

f. **Cleansing Incense (Good for Mental and Physical Well-Being)**
   - Sweetgrass is believed to support good vibes and purification.

- Blue Sage is believed to support money-healing and abundance.
- Rosemary is believed to support clarity and motivation.
- White Sage is believed to cleanse places, people, and energy crystals.
- Yerba Santa is believed to support self-love and growth.
- Juniper is believed to reset energy and offer stress relief.
- Palo Santo is believed to support peace, harmony, health, and luck.
- Cedar is believed to support confidence and strength.

III. **Meditation:** Meditation might feel impossible when you first start, but, as with most things, practice makes perfect. Be patient and start with five minutes. Increase each week's meditation by five minutes, until you can meditate for a minimum of twenty minutes.

a. Try to meditate **three times per day**—when you wake up, around noon, and before going to sleep for the day.

b. During your early morning meditation, try to **practice visualization**—identify the three most important things you need to accomplish that day and picture what it looks like to have done them.

c. Start each meditative session with a series of **long and slow inhales and exhales** and continue doing this while you close your eyes throughout the session.

d. Engage your senses.
   – **Sound:** In the morning, I listen to *432 Hz Pure Tones* because it activates my body chakras. While it plays, I use the time to reflect on things I feel good about and to plan for the day. Before I go to bed, I meditate to *Weightless*, which can be downloaded from any music source such as iTunes; the frequency helps your body relax and causes your brain to be at ease.
   – **Sight:** Face the sun or burn a candle, leaving your eyes open or closed. If your eyes are open, do not look directly into the sun! I found that closing my eyes in the beginning was helpful.
   – **Smell:** Burn frankincense, myrrh, palo santo, or sage.
   – **Touch:** Hold crystals that channel different energies.
      – *Rose:* channels love, hope, compassion
      – *Citrine:* channels creativity and prosperity
      – *Carnelian:* channels motivation

- *Green Aventurine:* channels abundance
- *Black Tourmaline:* channels protection and grounding

IV. **Preparation for an Optimal Day:** I am big into routine. Routine is important because if you can decrease the amount of time you spend making mundane decisions, you can channel more of your energy toward what really matters. Below is some insight into my routine.

a. Get six to eight hours of **sleep** (without any noise or interruption).

b. **Drink** a minimum of six ounces of water immediately when you wake up.

c. Choose and **prepare** (wash, mend, iron) **your clothes** the day before.

d. **Plan** what you're going to eat for breakfast the night before.

e. **Schedule** emails for the following day—this has helped me save a ton of time. Review your calendar for the next day; factor in driving time and down time so you can be punctual.

f. Block a minimum of one hour for **strategic planning and uninterrupted thinking** on your calendar for the week.

Chapter 6

I. **Traveling and Learning for Free (Fellowships, Grants, and International Programs):** I mentioned this in passing in the chapter, but I wanted to highlight just how many opportunities exist to travel abroad for free or on a limited budget. Below is a non-exhaustive list of programs, in no specific order, that I've either participated in personally or heard about from credible sources.

a. **The International Visitor Leadership Program (IVLP)**—US Department of State's premier professional exchange program.

b. **Atlantik-Bruecke German-American Young Leaders**—A comprehensive exchange and discussion program that connects young leaders from Germany and the United States.

c. **European Union Visitors Programme (EUVP)**—Invites young leaders from outside the European Union for study visits to the European institutions.

d. **BMW Foundation Herbert Quandt**—Promotes responsible leadership and inspires leaders world-wide to work toward a peaceful, just, and sustainable future.

e. **French-American Foundation Young Leaders**—Brings together leaders from different backgrounds, all in the name of forging bonds between France and the United States.

f. **The American Swiss Foundation**—Connects, informs, and engages Swiss and American leaders through innovative and inspirational programs to strengthen shared values of liberty, the rule of law, and free enterprise.

g. **The German Marshall Fund of the United States**—Nonpartisan American public policy think tank and grant-making institution dedicated to promoting cooperation and understanding between North America and Europe.

h. **American Council of Young Political Leaders (ACYPL)**—Premier organization for introducing rising political leaders and policymakers to international affairs and to one another.

i. **The Aspen Institute**—More than fifty programs gather diverse, nonpartisan thought leaders, creatives, scholars, and members of the public to address some of the world's most complex problems.

j. **Atlantic Council**—American think tank in the field of international affairs; founded in 1961, it provides a forum for international political, business, and intellectual leaders.

k. **IDEX Global Fellowship**—Program founded on the idea that by investing in the future generations of leaders who are passionate about having high-impact careers, people can regenerate local economies and build stronger communities around the world.

l. **Institute of International Education**—Organization that focuses on international student exchange and aid, foreign affairs, and international peace and security by creating programs of study and training for students, educators, and professionals from various sectors.

m. **The Robert Bosch Foundation Fellowship Program**—Transatlantic initiative that offers a select cohort of accomplished Americans the opportunity to complete a comprehensive intercultural professional program in Germany that is comprised of three main components: individual professional assignments, professional seminars, and German language training.

n. **Truman National Security Project**—National security and leadership development organization based in Washington, DC, serving to organize American progressives on issues of national security and foreign policy.

o. **Rotary Foundation Group Study Exchange**— Cultural and vocational exchange opportunity for businesspeople and professionals between the ages of twenty-five and forty who are in the early stages of their careers; provides travel grants for teams to exchange visits in paired areas of different countries.

p. **Cultural Vistas**—Organization that facilitates internships and professional exchange programs and services for visitors to the US, along with American students and professionals seeking experiential learning opportunities abroad.

CPSIA information can be obtained
at www.ICGtesting.com
Printed in the USA
LVHW110407180121
676770LV00030B/683/J